Cool, Calm and Confident

A Workbook to Help Kids Learn Assertiveness Skills

LISA M. SCHAB, LCSW

Instant Help Books

A Division of New Harbinger Publications, Inc.

Publisher's Note

Distributed in Canada by Raincoast Books

Copyright © 2009 by Lisa M. Schab
        Instant Help Books
        A Division of New Harbinger Publications, Inc.
        5674 Shattuck Avenue
        Oakland, CA 94609
        www.newharbinger.com

Cover design by Amy Shoup
Illustrated by Julie Olson
All photographs are of models used for illustrative purposes only

Printed in the United States of America

Library of Congress Cataloging-in-Publication Data

Schab, Lisa M.
Cool, calm, and confident : a workbook to help kids learn assertiveness skills / Lisa M. Schab.
    p. cm.
Includes bibliographical references.
ISBN-13: 978-1-57224-630-0 (pbk. : alk. paper)
ISBN-10: 1-57224-630-8 (pbk. : alk. paper)
ISBN-13: 978-1-57224-670-6 (pbk. with cd : alk. paper)
ISBN-10: 1-57224-670-7 (pbk. with cd : alk. paper)
  1. Assertiveness in children. I. Title.
BF723.A74S33 2009
649'.64--dc22

                              2008052313

FSC
www.fsc.org
MIX
Paper from
responsible sources
FSC® C011935

20   19   18

15   14   13   12

Contents

Introduction   v

Activity 1:   Three Communication Styles   1

Activity 2:   Your Thoughts Affect Your Actions   6

Activity 3:   The Golden Rule   10

Activity 4:   You Are Special   13

Activity 5:   Your Special Inner Qualities   17

Activity 6:   The Things You Do Well   21

Activity 7:   SMILE to Make Improvements   25

Activity 8:   Turn It Around   30

Activity 9:   The Picture of Assertiveness   33

Activity 10: An Assertive Attitude   37

Activity 11: Try, Try Again   41

Activity 12: Setting Small, Achievable Goals   46

Activity 13: Doing Things for Yourself   50

Activity 14: All About You   55

Activity 15: Your Values   60

Activity 16: Knowing Your Feelings   63

Activity 17: Managing Your Feelings   66

Activity 18: Staying Calm   71

Activity 19: Managing Your Anger   76

Activity 20: Choosing Real Friends   80

Activity 21: Taking Responsibility for Your Actions   86

Activity 22: Your Right to Say No   90

Activity 23: Your Rights   95

Activity 24: "I Feel" Statements   99

Activity 25: Starting a Conversation   105

Activity 26: Accepting and Giving Compliments   109

Activity 27: Assertiveness with a Group   114

Activity 28: Assertiveness with Adults   117

Activity 29: Separating People from Problems   123

Activity 30: Seeing Another Person's Point of View   127

Activity 31: Seeing Your Part in the Problem   131

Activity 32: CATTS Problem-Solving Guidelines   134

Activity 33: Brainstorming Solutions   139

Activity 34: Problem Solving Through Compromise   145

Activity 35: Playful Teasing and Harmful Teasing   149

Activity 36: Behaviors That Encourage or Discourage Teasing   153

Activity 37: SAIL Through Teasing   157

Activity 38: Staying Calm to Handle Teasing   161

Activity 39: When to Call for Help   166

Activity 40: Putting It All Together   170

Introduction

Dear Reader,

You are going to meet all different kinds of people in your life. Some you will want to be friends with, and some you won't. Some will be easy to get along with, and some will be difficult. Some will treat you with kindness and respect, and some will treat you rudely or unfairly.

You will discover that there is usually not much you can do to change other people or to make them act just the way you want them to. But when you use your energy to work on your own behavior, you can experience great success in getting along with others.

One of the best ways to get along with people is to learn how to act assertively. This means that you speak and act in ways that help you protect your rights but that you consider other people's rights as well. It means that you treat yourself with respect and you also treat other people with respect. Acting assertively isn't necessarily something you are born with, but it is something you can learn.

It is easier to have the strength and courage to act assertively when you feel good about yourself inside. Many of the activities in this workbook are designed to help you recognize your self-worth, your strengths, and your right to stand up for yourself.

Part of acting assertively is communicating with others in a positive and fair way—listening as much as you speak, expressing your feelings in an appropriate way, and using good manners. It also means solving problems and settling disagreements by using skills like taking responsibility for your actions and seeing things from another person's point of view. Activities in this workbook can teach you how to do this.

Many kids are teased about one thing or another at some time in their lives. When you act assertively, you can handle playful teasing without letting it bother you too much. You can also disarm harmful teasing by asking others for help. If you are a person who acts aggressively by bullying or teasing other kids, the activities in this workbook can teach you how to communicate in more caring and mature ways, and help you do a better job of making and keeping true friends.

This workbook teaches ideas and skills, but you must practice them and put them into action in order for them to work. If you think of learning assertiveness like any other subject you study, you know that you will get out of it as much as you put in. Be patient with yourself and keep trying, and you can succeed. Good luck!

Lisa M. Schab, LCSW

For You to Know

There are three main styles of talking and behaving that people use to communicate with each other: passive, aggressive, and assertive. The style that is considered the healthiest, the most fair, and the one that helps people get along with each other best is the assertive style.

When Passive Patsy wants something, she hints about it instead of asking directly. "I wish I had some yummy strawberries like you do," she whispers while she sits next to her friend at the lunch table.

Aggressive Aggie takes what she wants without asking. "Give me some of your strawberries!" she says loudly as she grabs some of her friend's berries.

Assertive Aser asks politely and directly for what he wants. "May I please have one of your strawberries?" he asks his friend. "I could trade you for some of my grapes."

Passive communicators like Patsy often sound whiny. They tend to say they agree with other people's ideas even if they really don't, but then they get mad when other people tell them what to do. They often complain about being unhappy and blame other people for it. They let others make decisions for them. They might feel like their opinions don't count.

Aggressive communicators like Aggie often sound mean, and they hurt other people in trying to get what they want. They may be argumentative and loud and put other people down. They can be insulting and cruel. They make decisions for other people without considering their feelings. They talk like their opinions are always right and there is no room for any other ideas.

Assertive communicators like Aser sound like they are trying to be fair. They say what they want, but they listen to and think about what other people want, too. They take responsibility for their thoughts, feelings, and actions without blaming others. They make decisions for themselves. They believe that their opinions count and so do other people's.

For You to Do

Patsy, Aggie, and Aser all want to swing on the swings, but other kids are already on them. Circle in yellow all the statements you think Patsy would say. Circle in red all the statements you think Aggie would say. Circle in blue all the statements you think Aser would say.

I just won't swing today.

I'd like to swing. Is anyone almost done?

Those kids are mean for not letting me swing.

You've been on there long enough. Get off!

May I swing when you're done?

Do you want to take turns swinging?

It's my turn, so move over!

Get off that swing now!

I don't deserve to swing anyway.

Circle the name of the child you'd most like to be friends with, and tell why.

Patsy   Aggie   Aser

_____

_____

Circle the name of the child who is most likely to get into trouble, and tell why.

Patsy   Aggie   Aser

_____

_____

Circle the name of the child or children you'd like to invite to your birthday party, and tell why.

Patsy   Aggie   Aser

_____

_____

Circle the name of the child you think is most likely to get to swing first, and tell why.

Patsy   Aggie   Aser

_____

_____

Circle the name of the child you think is most likely to get to swing last, and tell why.

Patsy   Aggie   Aser

_____

_____

...And More to Do!

Look at the following pictures and read the statements that describe how the children might respond. Next to each statement, write "P" if you think it is an example of passive communication, "AG" if you think it is an example of aggressive communication, or "AS" if you think it is an example of assertive communication.

"Hey, gimme that pencil!"

"Thanks for sharing your pencil."

"My pencil broke and I don't know what to do."

"I wish we could watch cartoons instead of this."

"Get rid of this show. I'm watching cartoons."

"Can we watch cartoons when this show is over?"

"I'm sorry. I wasn't watching what I was doing."

"Oh no, help! I'm so klutzy."

"Who told you to sit there, dummy!"

Pretend that your job is to be a communications observer. Use the following chart or make one like it. For the next day or two, write down the names of people you see and record whether you think they are communicating passively, aggressively, or assertively. Write at least one statement they use that helps you choose your answer.

Name	Passive	Aggressive	Assertive	What They Said

Activity 2

Your Thoughts Affect Your Actions

For You to Know

People's actions are influenced by the way they think and feel. If they think happy thoughts, they tend to act in happy ways. If they think unhappy thoughts, they tend to act in unhappy ways. It is easier to communicate in a healthy assertive style when you are thinking happy thoughts.

Bart, Ben, and Betty are triplets. They look a lot alike, but most of the time they don't act alike. Every morning, Bart feels a little scared. He doesn't like going to school because he is afraid the other kids won't like him. He also worries that they might make fun of him if they know he is afraid. When Bart arrives at the playground, he is thinking a lot of unhappy thoughts about being rejected. He is afraid that if he asks to join in the softball game, the kids will say no. So instead of asking, he just grabs another child's catcher's mitt and says loudly, "Now it's *my* turn to be catcher!" The other kids think Bart is mean, but they are afraid of him, so they let him play.

Ben is as scared as Bart. Sometimes he lies in bed so long that he misses the school bus. His mom gets mad because she has to drive him to school, which makes her late for work. He doesn't like going to school because he is afraid the other kids will make fun of him or not want to be friends with him. When Ben arrives at the playground, he is thinking a lot of unhappy thoughts about being rejected. He worries that if he asks to join in the softball game, the kids will say no. So instead of asking, he sits down under a tree at the edge of the field. A girl who notices Ben thinks because he is just sitting there, he doesn't want to play. Ben thinks no one likes him because no one asks him to play.

Betty is concerned about making friends, too. She wants kids to like her and sometimes worries that they won't, but she thinks happy thoughts. She knows that she is a nice person and that if she acts nicely, kids should want to be around her. Even though she feels a little scared, she puts on a smile and feels hopeful that she will have a good day. When she arrives at the playground, she is thinking about what fun she might have. She wonders if the other kids will let her join in the softball game, so she taps one boy's shoulder, smiles at him, and asks if it's all right if she plays. The boy sees her friendly smile, and says, "Sure. You can get in line to bat."

For You to Do

Think about how Bart, Betty, and Ben each handled the situation with the softball game. Then answer the questions under each child's name.

Bart

Why do you think Bart acted so meanly or aggressively? _____

_____

How do you think Bart feels about himself? _____

_____

What do you think the other kids think about Bart? _____

_____

What thoughts would have made Bart feel better and act differently? _____

_____

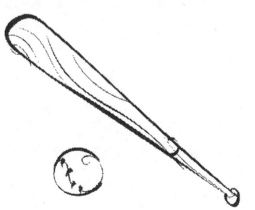

Ben

Why do you think Ben acted so meekly or passively? _____

_____

How do you think Ben feels about himself? _____

_____

What do you think the other kids think about Ben? _____

_____

What thoughts would have made Ben feel better and act differently?

_____

_____

Betty

Why do you think Betty acted so nicely or assertively? _____

_____

How do you think Betty feels about herself? _____

_____

What do you think the other kids think about Betty? _____

_____

What thoughts did Betty have that made her feel good and act nicely? _____

_____

... *And More to Do*

What kinds of thoughts can you tell yourself that would help you feel happy about yourself? Write three examples here.

_____

_____

_____

What kinds of thoughts can you tell yourself that would help you feel unhappy about yourself? Write three examples here.

_____

_____

_____

When you are thinking happy thoughts about yourself, it is easier to feel good about yourself, make friends, and get along with others. It is easier to stand up for yourself, feel equal to others, and act assertively, respecting your own rights and those of other people, too.

Pretend you are approaching a group of kids with whom you'd like to play. Write some happy thoughts that could make you feel good about yourself and the kids.

_____

_____

Tell how you could speak or act assertively to see if you can play with them.

_____

_____

For You to Know

Being assertive is a combination of treating both yourself and other people nicely and with respect. Some people call this idea the Golden Rule and say it like this: "Treat other people the way you want to be treated yourself." Understanding and remembering the Golden Rule can help you know how to act assertively.

Holly was moving to another town. She was feeling both excited and scared about starting at a new school. She hoped she would meet some nice kids to play with, but she was unsure about how to make new friends.

Holly told her mother how she was feeling, and her mother said all she needed to do was remember the Golden Rule. Together they repeated the rule: *"Treat other people the way you want to be treated yourself."*

"How would you like kids to treat you?" asked her mother.

"I'd like them to be friendly," said Holly. "I'd like them to come up and introduce themselves and ask me to play with them. I'd like them to make me feel welcome. I'd like them to give me a chance to be friends with them."

"Well," said Holly's mother, "then that is exactly the way you should treat them. Be friendly toward them; go up and introduce yourself and ask if they'd like to play with you. Make them feel welcome and give them a chance to be friends with you."

When Holly went to her new school on the first day, she wore a small gold ring that reminded her to use the Golden Rule. When she treated the new kids the way she would want them to treat her, she found that they treated her the same way. Holly met lots of nice kids that day and made new friends. "That Golden Rule really works!" she told her mother. "I'm going to use it for the rest of my life!"

For You to Do

On the first line below each picture, write something one child could say to the other that would be an example of following the Golden Rule. On the second line, write something that child could do that would be an example of following the Golden Rule.

_____

_____

_____

_____

_____

_____

_____

_____

... *And More to Do*

Circle the words below that describe how you would like other people to treat you. Use the blank lines to add more ideas of your own if you'd like.

Ignore me.	Smile at me.	Hurt my feelings.
Be polite.	Be nice.	Be patient with me.
Be thoughtful.	Be rude.	Ask me to play with them.
Shut me out.	Tease me meanly.	Apologize if they hurt me.
Be friendly.	Make fun of me.	Tell my secrets.
Be bossy.	Share with me.	Push me around.
Be kind.	Have fun with me.	Make mean faces at me.
Tell lies about me.	Invite me to join them.	Show me they like me.
_____	_____	_____

Look at the words you circled. Are these ways you treat other people? Describe one time when you treated someone in a way that follows the Golden Rule.

_____

_____

How do you think people will react to you when you follow the Golden Rule?

_____

_____

How do you think people will react to you when you do not follow the Golden Rule?

_____

_____

For You to Know

People are like snowflakes—no two are exactly alike. People all have their own positive qualities that make them special and important. No matter what your name is, where you live, what you look like, what you have, or what you do, there is only one you.

If you look outside at the natural world, you will find a great deal of diversity. Although there are many maple trees, no two are exactly alike. Although there are many robins, each one is a little different from the others. Although there are new clouds floating in the sky each day, never are any two exactly the same.

The diversity we find in nature is purposeful and helpful. Different kinds of plants and animals, different landforms and weather, all combine to make the world work as perfectly as it does. Rain is for watering, sun is for warming and lighting, wind scatters seeds, and snow provides a blanket for the earth in winter. If there weren't such great diversity, our planet couldn't survive.

The same is true for people. Each person has a special purpose and brings something unique to the world. One may have good farming skills and provide us with food. Another may have good singing skills and provide us with music. Some people provide us with health care when we are sick; some help us find books at the library when we want to read. Some people brighten our lives with their laughter, and some keep us warm with their love.

No matter who you are, you are special. Knowing this fact can help you have the confidence to take care of yourself by acting and speaking in your best interest. Knowing that everyone else is also special can help you care about their rights too, even if they are very different from you. When you act assertively, you are speaking and acting in both your and other people's best interests.

For You to Do

Use some type of washable paint to paint the palm of your hand. When your palm is completely covered with paint, press it onto the space in the first frame below. If you cannot use paint, spread your fingers apart and press one hand into the space below. Then using your other hand, trace around your fingers and palm to make an outline of your hand. You can also have someone else trace your hand for you.

Cool, Calm, and Confident

Paste a photograph of yourself at any age in the second frame. If you don't have a photograph, you can draw a picture of yourself in the space.

Look at the pictures in both frames. No one else in the whole world has the same handprint or the same face and body that you do. Even if a million children did this same activity, each one would be different, because no two children are alike. Each child is special and brings a special personality to the world.

... And More to Do

Write the name of your best friend. Then write four things that make you different from that friend.

_____

1._____   3._____

2._____   4._____

Write the name of someone who is your same age and gender. Then write four things that make you different from that person.

1._____   3._____

2._____   4._____

Write the name of someone who is most like you in the whole world. Then write four things that make you different from that person.

1._____   3._____

2._____   4._____

Tell what you think it would be like if all your friends were exactly like you.

_____

_____

_____

Tell something that is very special about you.

_____

_____

_____

For You to Know

The most important part of you is the part that you don't see. This is the part of you that makes up your personality and the positive inner qualities you use when you relate to other people. Thinking about these qualities can help you build your confidence so that you can choose to act assertively.

When Jaxson looked in the mirror, he didn't like everything he saw. He thought his nose was too big and stuck out too far. He didn't like the part of his hair that would never lie flat. He thought he had too many freckles.

Jaxson's grandfather saw him looking in the mirror with a sad face and asked what was wrong. "There's nothing good about me," Jaxson answered.

"Oh my!" said his grandfather as he put an arm around Jaxson. "You're looking for yourself in the wrong place. To find the really important parts of you, you've got to look on the inside."

"How can I do that?" asked Jaxson.

"First, close your eyes," said his grandfather. "Then pay attention to your heart. Not the organ that beats in your chest, but the heart of who you are. Look for all the good that you see there. For example, I see that you are a very kind boy. I see you share your toys with your friends. I see you help your mother feed your baby sister, even when you'd rather be doing something else. I see you caring for the sick bird that you found in your backyard. Those are the things that are the most important, but you can't see them when you look in the mirror."

Jaxson thought about what his grandfather said. He knew it was true. When he closed his eyes and looked inside himself, he saw things that were more important than how many freckles he had. This made him feel better about himself. He also knew that it was the same for other people, too. The most important part of people was not the way they looked, but the things that made them nice to be around.

For You to Do

Circle any of the words or phrases below that describe your special inner qualities—things you can't see when you look in the mirror.

kind	happy	generous	smart
loving	good at sharing	fun to be with	polite
honest	loyal	trying my best	caring
trustworthy	obedient	courteous	sincere
a good friend	funny	lighthearted	nice
helpful	hardworking	thoughtful	affectionate
considerate	unselfish	a good listener	dependable
responsible	gentle	sympathetic	flexible
open	respectful	cheerful	law abiding

In the frame below, draw an outline of your body. Make it big enough so that you can write inside it. Copy all the words you circled into the outline to show what you look like on the inside. Use your favorite colors to fill in the empty space.

My Special Inner Qualities

... *And More to Do*

Choose three of your special inner qualities and describe a time when you could use each of them to treat yourself and other people with respect. For example, if you are kind, tell about a situation where you could show kindness to yourself and others. Put a star next to the special inner quality you are most proud of.

My Qualities	When I Could Use Them

The more positive inner qualities we have, the better we can feel about ourselves. Look back at the earlier list and write down qualities you didn't circle but would like to work on acquiring or increasing. For example, if you would like to become a hard worker, write that down. If you would like to become more caring than you are now, write that down.

_____

_____

_____

Tell some specific ways you can practice increasing or acquiring these qualities. For example, to increase your sharing, you could let a friend borrow a toy from you; to increase your helpfulness, you could offer to wash the dishes for your parents.

_____

_____

_____

For You to Know

Everyone has special talents. These are things that come easily to you and that you do well. When you think about and do these things, you feel good about yourself. Thinking about your talents can help you build your confidence so you can choose to act assertively.

Madison's Girl Scout troop was working on the cooking badge. Madison had cooked with her mother at home a few times, but she had always made mistakes that ruined the meal. She was sure she would make mistakes at the troop meeting, too. She thought about it over and over again and made herself scared.

At the meeting, Madison sat at the back of the room while the rest of the girls were measuring ingredients and stirring things in bowls. Mrs. Gress, the troop leader, asked her what was wrong. "I'm not good at cooking," said Madison. "They'll probably laugh at me."

"Well," said Mrs. Gress, "tell me what you are good at." Madison thought a minute and then answered, "Skiing." "Then that is what you should focus on," said Mrs. Gress. "If we think only about the things we aren't good at, we will feel bad about ourselves. If we think about the things we are good at, we can feel good about ourselves. Tell me about how you ski." Madison said, "I started out on the beginner slopes, but now I'm good enough to go on the bigger ones with my parents. I love riding the ski lift and going really fast. And I hardly ever fall!" Now Madison had a big smile on her face.

"Keep thinking about how good you are at skiing," said Mrs. Gress. "And then go join the other girls. Just do what you feel comfortable with—maybe measure one ingredient. Then watch and learn, or help to clean up. Everybody has things they excel at and things they need help with. Remember the things you're good at and you'll feel better about yourself."

For You to Do

Below each trophy are lines for you to write things that you are good at. Think about everything you do well, and give yourself a trophy for each talent or skill you have. Maybe you know how to be gentle with animals, or maybe you are good at keeping your room clean. Maybe you are a good brother or the best speller in the class or can jump really high. Write down each talent you have, and use more paper if you need to.

Draw a star on each of the three trophies that tell what you do the *very* best.

Cool, Calm, and Confident

... And More to Do

Try to add three more things to your skill list. If you can't think of anything else, ask a friend or family member to help you. Remember, *everything* counts—even getting to school on time!

1. _____

2. _____

3. _____

Look at your list of skills and talents. Tell how you feel about yourself when you think about all the things you do well.

_____

_____

Remember that everyone is good at something, not just you. The child who gets picked last for the basketball team might be really good at whistling. The child who fails the science test might be a great secret-keeper. Focusing on both your strengths and other people's strengths can help you act assertively, because you believe in yourself and other people as well.

Tell three things that your best friend is good at.

1. _____

2. _____

3. _____

Tell three things that your parent is good at.

1. _____

2. _____

3. _____

Think of someone you don't like very much. Tell three things that person is good at.

1. _____

2. _____

3. _____

Think of someone who other kids make fun of at school. Tell three things that person is good at.

1. _____

2. _____

3. _____

For You to Know

No one is perfect. No one does everything well. We all have areas that we need help with and need to improve upon. Accepting these challenges and trying our best to meet them can help us feel better about ourselves. When we feel good about ourselves, it is easier for us to act assertively.

The greatest athlete in the world may have trouble with reading. The smartest scientist may have a terrible singing voice. The doctor who saves many lives might fall off of a bike every time she gets on.

We all know about some area of our lives where we could use improvement. This doesn't mean there is anything wrong with us; it just means we are normal human beings. There will always be places where we need to improve, but if we let our weaknesses bother us, we will always be unhappy. The best way to deal with weaknesses is with a SMILE:

S   See them

M   Manage them

I   Improve them

L   Let them go

E   Expect things to get better

We have to first **SEE** our weaknesses before we have a chance of changing them. In gym class, Shawna tried playing sports and could **SEE** that she needed help catching a ball. Steve thought he might not be good at sports and said he was sick so that he could get out of gym class. He never gave himself the chance to change.

When we know we need help in a certain area, we must **MANAGE** it so it doesn't get worse. Marc saw that he needed help with multiplication, so he asked his older brother to go over his math homework with him every week. That helped him **MANAGE** his work and kept him from making more mistakes. Marissa saw that she needed help with math, but she didn't do anything about it. Her grades got worse and worse.

Working to **IMPROVE** our weaknesses can make them better. Izzy practiced playing the trumpet every afternoon. This **IMPROVED** his playing enough that he could join the band. Ingrid told her trumpet teacher that she was having a hard time, but she didn't want to practice. She wanted the teacher to give her easier music to play, but that didn't make her a better player.

Once we have seen our weaknesses, managed them, and tried our best to improve them, it is time to **LET THEM GO.** Sitting around thinking about how bad we are at something never makes us any better. Logan tried to improve his social skills by saying hi to more kids at school, but he spent so much time worrying about his shyness that he got stomachaches. Lynda wanted to make more friends, too. She practiced saying hi to more kids at school, and then she **LET IT GO** from her mind and thought about something else, like how much fun she was going to have at the carnival. Because she let go of her worry, she was happier, and the kids she said hi to responded to her better.

Our thoughts create our experiences. If we expect ourselves to fail, we will. If we **EXPECT THINGS TO GET BETTER,** they will. Elizabeth knew she needed help with her dance steps and tried to improve, but in her mind she still thought of herself as clumsy. Because she thought this way, she never put her heart into practice, and she never did improve. Eva knew she needed help with her dance steps and tried to improve. In her mind, she **EXPECTED THINGS TO GET BETTER.** She believed that her extra practice would pay off. This made her determined and focused when she practiced, and she did get better.

For You to Do

In the frame below, draw a picture of something you need to improve at.

Start using the **SMILE** method by answering the following questions.

What do you **SEE** that you need to improve at?

_____

_____

How can you **MANAGE** this so things don't get worse?

_____

_____

What can you do to try to **IMPROVE** your skill?

_____

_____

Are you willing to **LET GO** of thinking about your weakness and think happy thoughts?

_____

_____

Tell how you **EXPECT THINGS TO GET BETTER.**

_____

_____

... And More to Do

Many people frown and get discouraged when they think about the things they are not good at. This makes them tired and sad, and they don't have much energy for making things better. If you smile when you think of the things you need to improve, you will feel better about yourself and have more energy for making things better.

Next to each smiley face below, describe something else you would like to improve about yourself. For each, make a SMILE plan for it, or tell what you can do to improve it.

☺ _____

_____

_____

_____

☺ _____

_____

_____

_____

☺ _____

_____

_____

_____

Describe how you will feel when you improve any one of these things.

_____

_____

For You to Know

Everyone makes mistakes. That is why there are erasers on pencils. If you think about a mistake as an opportunity to improve something, you don't have to feel upset about it. Accepting your mistakes and then turning the experience around to see it positively can help you feel good about yourself. When you feel good about yourself, you are better able to act assertively.

After Isaac was caught throwing water balloons at cars, a police officer came to talk to him and his parents. "Interfering with someone's driving is dangerous," he said. "Someone could have been hurt or killed." Isaac felt terrible. He had been having fun but hadn't realized how much damage he could have done.

The officer told Isaac he would have to do twenty hours of community service to make up for his actions. Isaac's parents said that they were shocked at his behavior, but they also had confidence that he could turn this mistake around.

"Mistakes are part of being human," his father explained, "and they are also chances to turn something negative around and make it positive. Can you think of a way to do that through your community service?" "I could volunteer at the hospital and then I'd be helping people instead of hurting them," Isaac said. "Good idea," said his dad.

At the hospital that summer, Isaac pushed a snack cart down the halls for the patients. He read books to people who were lonely and played checkers with people who were bored. Sometimes he cleaned up spills and washed floors. Isaac worked hard at his job, arriving on time every day and being as kind as he could to the patients.

At the end of the summer, the head nurse told Isaac that he had been one of the best volunteers they ever had, and everyone was thankful for his hard work and kindness. Isaac's parents were proud of him, and Isaac was proud of himself, too. "I know I'll make more mistakes in my life," admitted Isaac. "But I'm going to try to turn them all around into something positive."

For You to Do

Each picture below shows a kid who has made a mistake. On the blank lines, write what these kids could do to make up for their actions and feel better about themselves.

... And More to Do

Describe a mistake you made recently.

_____

_____

_____

How did you feel about yourself when you made this mistake?

_____

_____

_____

Describe something you did, or could have done, to try to turn this mistake around or correct it.

_____

_____

_____

How did you, or would you, feel about yourself if you turned the mistake around into something positive?

_____

_____

_____

The Picture of Assertiveness

For You to Know

People who are assertive have certain things in common about the way they look and act. Their self-assurance shows in their faces, in the way they hold their bodies, and in their movements. Their manner and look is welcoming and inviting to others and reflects their self-confidence.

When people feel confident in themselves, you can see it from the first time you look at them. People who are acting **assertively** will usually:

- Smile in a friendly way when they meet you

- Hold out their hand to shake yours

- Have a bright, positive look in their eyes

- Look happy and content

- Look into your eyes when they speak to you

- Stand tall, using good posture

- Look healthy

- Be clean and well groomed

- Appear comfortable to be with you

People who are acting **passively** will usually look more timid, look down instead of into your eyes, appear uncomfortable, slouch or droop their shoulders, and seem to have a low amount of energy.

People who are acting **aggressively** will usually look more intimidating, look at you forcefully, push their bodies too close to yours or make you feel like backing away from them, and appear to have excess energy that they direct toward you.

For You to Do

In these boxes, paste pictures of people who look assertive, passive, and aggressive.
You may cut these out of old magazines or newspapers, or use old photographs that
no one wants. Be sure to get permission before you cut out these pictures. If you don't
have any pictures to cut out, draw your own.

Assertive Looks

Passive Looks

Aggressive Looks

... And More to Do

Reread the information on what assertiveness looks like. Stand in front of a mirror, or another person, and practice using your face and body to look assertive:

- Put on a smile.

- Stand up tall and use good posture.

- Hold your chin straight.

- Relax your muscles so you feel calm.

- Look into the eyes of the person in front of you.

- Repeat a positive thought in your head to help yourself feel confident.

Write how you feel inside when you look this way.

_____

Next, change your look to pretend you are acting passively:

- Lose your smile.

- Slouch and droop your shoulders a little.

- Drop your chin.

- Look down.

- Think a negative thought about yourself.

Write how you feel inside when you look this way.

_____

Finally, change your look to pretend you are acting aggressively:

- Put a hostile look on your face.

- Tense your jaw.

- Stare meanly.

- Stick your chin out forcefully.

- Lean forward as if you are looking for a fight.

- Think an angry thought about the person you are looking at.

Write how you feel inside when you look this way.

_____

Now go back to your assertive appearance. Close your eyes and feel what it feels like in your body to hold an assertive pose. Practice holding your body this way when you want to feel good about yourself and about other people, too.

For You to Know

When you choose to have a positive attitude, you see the good in yourself, in others, and in every situation. You expect a good outcome and you act in ways that will achieve that outcome. This approach helps you feel confident rather than scared and gives you the courage to act assertively.

Every day Annemarie hoped that someone would notice how lonely she was and ask her to play. But no one ever seemed to notice, except for Annemarie's teacher, who asked, "Why are you sitting by yourself?"

"Because my best friend moved and none of the other kids wants to play with me," Annemarie answered.

"If you keep telling yourself that, you won't ever make new friends," said her teacher. "I think it's time to change the way you think. Let's write down some of the thoughts you are thinking right now."

Annemarie's list looked like this:

I am too shy to make new friends.

No one wants to be friends with me.

I won't ever have more friends.

I don't know what to say to people.

"These thoughts are all negative," explained her teacher. "How can you change these words so that they are positive?" Annemarie looked at her list and rewrote her thoughts so they were positive.

I am not too shy to make new friends.

Lots of kids want to be friends with me.

I will make new friends.

I can think of things to say to people.

"How do you feel when you look at your first list?" asked the teacher.

"Bad about myself and sad," answered Annemarie.

"And how do you feel when you look at your second list?"

"Really good about myself and excited to meet some new kids," said Annemarie.

"Well, then," said the teacher, "put those positive thoughts into your head and go make some friends."

For You to Do

The kids in the pictures below are thinking negative thoughts that make them feel bad and make it hard for them to act assertively. Help them adjust their attitudes by writing new positive thoughts on the blank lines.

I could really use some help with this drawing, but I know David won't want to help me. He's too busy helping Sara.

I've got nothing to do, but those girls won't let me play with them.

_____

_____

_____

_____

_____

_____

_____

_____

_____

_____

_____

_____

... And More to Do

Think about something you would like to do but have been afraid to try. Maybe you want to be the class president or volunteer to read to little kids at the library. Maybe you have wanted to play softball but are afraid you wouldn't be any good. Write down all the negative thoughts you are having about this situation.

_____

_____

How do you feel about yourself when you read these thoughts?

_____

Now go back and cross out each negative thought, one by one, and write a new positive thought to replace it.

_____

_____

Read your new positive thoughts out loud. How do you feel now?

_____

Tell what might be scary about changing from negative to positive thoughts.

_____

_____

Tell what might be exciting about changing from negative to positive thoughts.

_____

_____

Try, Try Again

For You to Know

Success doesn't always come quickly or easily. People who attempt to do anything often have to try many times over before they actually succeed. If you are willing to try, try again even after you make mistakes, you can reach your goal and feel good about yourself.

Mr. Roth was teaching the fifth-grade class a lesson in being successful. He told them that a big part of being successful was being willing to try, try again, and try yet again when attempting to achieve something. "But I get tired of trying!" said Daniel.

"Yeah, it feels discouraging when I keep making mistakes," said Carina.

"Well, kids," replied Mr. Roth, "if you don't keep trying, you will miss out on a lot of success in your life. Remember Thomas Edison, who invented the light bulb? Well, the story goes that Thomas Edison tried at least *1,000* times before he was finally successful. What do you think would have happened if he had stopped trying because he was tired or discouraged after 50 tries—or 500 tries—or *800 tries?*"

"I guess I should keep trying to be a better basket shooter in gym class," said Daniel.

"Yes," said Carina, "I guess I should keep trying to be a better speller."

"That's right," said Mr. Roth. "If at first you don't succeed, try, try again. Being discouraged and quitting means that you definitely won't achieve your goal, but continuing to try means that you always have another chance at succeeding. When you are finally successful—even if you have to try 1,000 times—you will feel good about yourself, not only for your success, but for your perseverance, for never giving up."

For You to Do

The pictures below show other inventions that people did not figure out on the first try. They had to try, try again to get their inventions to work right and work well. Next to each invention, write its name and how the world would be different if the inventor had given up on creating it after one or two mistakes.

Cool, Calm, and Confident

_____
_____
_____
_____

_____
_____
_____
_____

_____
_____
_____
_____

... *And More to Do*

Think of all of the things you have learned to do since you were born, and make a list of them here. Write down every small and big success you have had. Your list can include everything from learning to feed yourself or talk to learning karate or a foreign language.

_____   _____

_____   _____

_____   _____

_____   _____

_____   _____

_____   _____

_____   _____

_____   _____

Now put a star next to any of your successes that you accomplished *the first time* you tried it. Put a double T ("TT") next to any of your successes that you had to try, try again to accomplish.

What would have happened if you had given up on these things because you didn't accomplish them on the first try?

_____

_____

_____

Circle the one success on your list that you are most proud of. Tell how you feel about achieving this success.

_____

_____

_____

Sometimes acting assertively by standing up for yourself can feel scary. Maybe you think you can't do it. You might try but not succeed the first time. Tell what will happen if you get discouraged and stop trying.

_____

_____

_____

Tell what will happen if you try, try again.

_____

_____

_____

Setting Small, Achievable Goals

For You to Know

The best way to succeed at something is to set small goals that you know you will be able to achieve. When you set goals that are too high or too difficult, you can become discouraged more easily and want to give up. Reaching your goals will help you feel good about yourself, and that will help give you the strength to act assertively.

Connor wanted to interview and videotape ten famous airline pilots for his history-of-flight project. He also planned to build a historic model airplane to go with each interview. His history teacher said it was a good idea, but she didn't know if it would be possible. Connor started to do research on the Internet, and found some names of pilots. But he felt frustrated when he learned that many of them lived far away or he could not find ways to contact them. Two of the pilots were deceased. Connor felt discouraged and wanted to give up. His mother said he had just set an unrealistic goal. She helped him rethink it. Connor decided to make three model planes, and write short biographies of the airline pilots who flew them instead. The project turned out well and Connor felt happy.

Jazmine had to do a science project. She wanted to make a moving solar system that showed how the planets revolved around the sun. Her dad knew a lot about electrical work, and he said he would help her. But when she told him that it was due the next day, he told her she had to rethink her goal. The one she had set was too big. There wouldn't be time to plan and execute such a complicated project in one day. She decided to use Styrofoam balls on sticks to show the planets. She painted the balls, put them on sticks, created a good project, and still got to bed on time. She felt good about achieving her goal.

For You to Do

Read the three situations described below. Help Alissa and Evan choose small, achievable goals that will keep them from feeling discouraged. Cross out the goals that are too big. Circle the goals that are smaller and achievable. Under each goal, tell what might happen if the child tries to achieve it.

Alissa wants to make friends.

Invite the whole class to her house for a party.

_____

_____

Smile and say hi to someone who looks friendly.

_____

_____

Bring a ball to the playground and ask someone to play catch with her.

_____

_____

Bring gifts to school for each child in her class.

_____

_____

Talk to someone in the cafeteria line and ask if she could sit with that kid at the lunch table.

_____

_____

Evan wants to be a great basketball player.

Ask for a basketball for his birthday so he can start to practice.

_____

_____

Hang out with other kids after school who want to shoot hoops with him.

_____

_____

Ask the coach if he can join the team right away.

_____

_____

Join a team of adults who used to be professional players.

_____

_____

Practice shooting baskets three times a week.

_____

_____

... And More to Do

Think of something you would like to accomplish in the next year. Write your goal below, and then write some small goals that can help you accomplish your bigger goal. For example, if your goal is to learn to swim, a small goal would be to ask your parents if you can take swim lessons.

My goal is _____.

Some small goals are _____

_____.

Think of something you would like to accomplish when you are a teenager. Write your goal below, and then write some small goals that can help you accomplish it.

My goal is _____.

Some small goals are _____

_____.

Think of something you would like to accomplish when you grow up. Write your goal below, and then write some small goals you will have to accomplish to achieve that larger goal. If you are not sure how to achieve this goal, ask an adult for help.

My goal is _____.

Some small goals are _____

_____.

Tell how you think you will feel when you achieve these goals.

_____

_____

_____

Activity 13   Doing Things for Yourself

For You to Know

When you do things for yourself, you are being independent. Acting independently can help you feel good about yourself. It can help you feel strong and confident so that it will be easier for you to act assertively.

At different ages, people can do different things for themselves. Small babies need a lot of help with most things. They need help being fed and bathed and burped and having their diapers changed. By the time they are in grade school, children have learned to do many things for themselves. They can get dressed, brush their own teeth, shower, read books, play games, and study many subjects at school. They can learn to ride bikes and swim and sing songs.

Sometimes it might feel nice to pretend you are still very small and have your parents do things for you. When you aren't feeling well, you might like them to tuck you under a blanket and bring you orange juice or homemade chicken soup. It feels good to be taken care of and loved like this.

But it also feels good to do things for yourself. You may find out that you can do more than you ever thought you could. While you are learning to act independently, it is important to know the difference between things that are safe to do by yourself and things that are not safe. You also have to keep the rules that your parents have made.

Becoming independent means that you are growing up and growing smart and strong. The more you can do for yourself, the better you will feel about yourself.

For You to Do

Draw a picture of yourself doing something you have learned to do that you are proud of. Write a title for your picture.

Draw a picture of yourself doing something you would like to learn to do someday. Write a title for your picture.

... And More to Do

Next to each activity, write the age you were when you learned how to do it. If you don't remember, you can ask a parent to remind you.

Eat with a spoon   _____

Walk by yourself   _____

Throw a ball   _____

Tie your own shoes   _____

Read by yourself   _____

Write your name   _____

Use a computer   _____

Go down a slide   _____

Swing on a swing   _____

Hit a baseball   _____

Next to each of these activities, write the age you think you will be when you learn how to do it. If you don't know, you can ask an adult to help you.

Live in your own house
of apartment   _____

Drive a car   _____

Use an ATM machine   _____

Vote in a state or national   _____
election

Work as a cashier at a store   _____

Tell what is the easiest thing you have ever learned to do. Why was it so easy?

_____

_____

_____

How did you feel about yourself when you learned to do this?

_____

_____

_____

Tell what is the hardest thing you have ever learned to do. Why was it so hard?

_____

_____

_____

How did you feel about yourself when you learned to do this?

_____

_____

_____

For You to Know

You are special and different from every other person. No one else has the same combination of thoughts, feelings, bones, and muscles as you do. Identifying the things that make you uniquely yourself can help you feel strong, sure, and able to act assertively.

The picture below shows some of the things that are just yours and no one else's.

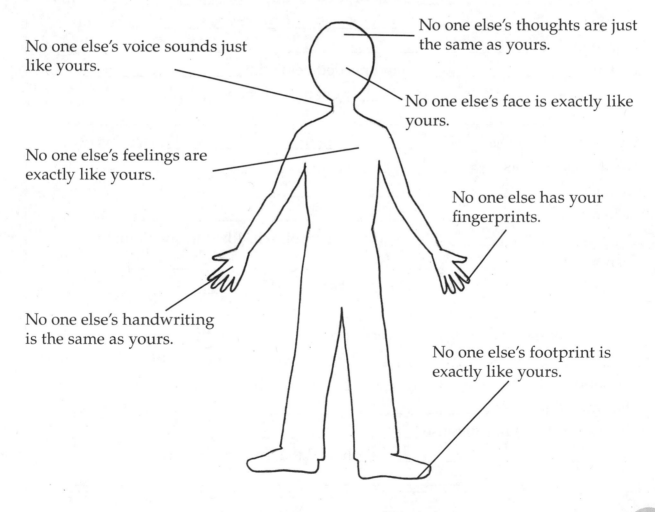

No one else's voice sounds just like yours.

No one else's thoughts are just the same as yours.

No one else's face is exactly like yours.

No one else's feelings are exactly like yours.

No one else has your fingerprints.

No one else's handwriting is the same as yours.

No one else's footprint is exactly like yours.

For You to Do

Pretend you are writing a short story about yourself and your life. Fill in the blank spaces with information about yourself.

Once upon a time there was a child named _____.
_____ was born on _____
and lived in the town of _____. S/he had
_____ hair and _____ eyes. S/he had _____
sisters and _____ brothers. The other people in her/his family were

_____.

_____'s favorite color was _____, her/his
favorite food was _____, and her/his
favorite toy was _____. This child was very
good at _____ and needed help with _____.
_____ went to the school named

_____.

Her/his favorite subject was _____. Her/his least
favorite subject was _____. Her/his
best friend was _____ and her/his favorite
teacher was _____. When
_____ wasn't in school, s/he liked to spend most of
her/his time _____.
When s/he went on vacation, s/he most liked to go to _____
because _____.

One of the best things that ever happened to this child was
_____. One of the most difficult things that
ever happened to this child was _____.
S/he wanted to be a _____ when s/he grew up.
S/he wanted to be this because _____.
_____ hoped that someday s/he could also

_____.

In the box below, draw a picture of yourself to go with your story. Think about the way you look that is different from everyone else. Show those special characteristics in your picture.

... *And More to Do*

Could the story above be about anyone else but you? Why or why not?

_____

_____

Think about other things you know about yourself, and answer these questions.

How long is your hair? _____

How tall are you? _____

Where are you ticklish? _____

What kinds of clothes do you usually wear? _____

_____

What do you like to do after school? _____

_____

What do you like to do on weekends? _____

_____

What do you like to do in summer? _____

_____

What do you like to do in winter? _____

_____

Who is your favorite person to spend time with? _____

What is your favorite outdoor game? _____

What is your favorite indoor game? _____

What is your favorite book? _____

What is your favorite TV show? _____

If you could make three wishes, what would they be?

1. _____

2. _____

3. _____

Write something else you know about yourself that wasn't asked here.

_____

_____

_____

For You to Know

Everyone has ideas about what it means to be a good person. These ideas are called values. When we make decisions about how to speak or act, we usually try to act in accordance with our values. Identifying your values helps you to know yourself. Acting assertively often involves standing up for your values.

Max and Sam were Cub Scouts. Their pack leader was teaching them about the laws they would be expected to learn and follow when they became Boy Scouts. "Why are there so many rules?" asked Max. "These rules are based on the Boy Scout values," explained the pack leader. "Values are standards we believe in that help us act in positive ways. Our values guide us every time we make a decision. For example, Sam, if you saw a handicapped man who needed help crossing the street, what would you do?" "I'd help him," Sam said. "Why?" asked the pack leader. "Because it's the nice thing to do," answered Sam. "So being nice to other people must be one of your values," said the pack leader. "Yes," Sam agreed. "I guess it is."

"I get it," said Max. "So cleaning my room is one of my mom's values!" "Something like that," said the pack leader. "Maybe she values cleanliness and order. Do you?" "Well," said Max, "I guess if I didn't clean my room it would get pretty awful. I guess I value cleanliness. I just wish I didn't have to clean my room."

"It sounds like you also value respecting your parents," said the pack leader. "You may not like cleaning your room, but you do it because your mother asks you to. That means respect is also one of your values. That is similar to one of the Boy Scout laws—obedience. A Boy Scout follows the rules of his family, school, pack, community, and country. If he doesn't like a rule, he tries to have it changed in an orderly manner instead of disobeying it."

For You to Do

The words below all represent ways of acting that people might value. Read each one and decide if it is something you value. If it is, put a check mark next to it. If you don't know what one of the words means, ask an adult to explain it to you.

____ honesty   ____ helpfulness   ____ kindness

____ courage   ____ cleanliness   ____ loyalty

____ obedience   ____ courtesy   ____ friendliness

Do you have any other values that weren't listed before? If so, write them here.

_____

_____

Tell what you would do in each of these situations, and then tell which of your values helped you decide what to do.

You are playing with your class on the playground at recess. A new girl who just joined your class is standing by herself at the door of the school. She looks lonely. What would you do? Which of your values helped you decide?

_____

_____

You and your brother are having a pillow fight. You throw the pillow and accidentally break a lamp. Your father hears the crash and comes in. Your brother has a pillow in his hands so it looks like he broke the lamp, not you. Your father gets angry and says to your brother, "You are going to be grounded for this!" What would you do? Which of your values helped you decide?

_____

_____

... And More to Do

We can stand up for our values by acting assertively. Read this story and answer the questions after it.

Meg was at the store with her friend Amy. The girls wanted a pack of gum, but neither of them had any money. Meg was wearing a jacket with big pockets. Amy said, "Just put the gum in your pocket. No one will know."

Meg didn't want to do that because stealing is dishonest and illegal. She acted assertively and stood up for her values. She told Amy, "No, I won't do that. I act honestly and obey the laws." Amy called Meg a chicken, and both girls left the store.

What were Meg's values?

_____

_____

Do you think it was easy for her to stand up for them?

_____

_____

How do you think she felt when Amy called her a chicken?

_____

_____

How do you think she felt knowing she had stood up for her values?

_____

_____

For You to Know

People have many different feelings. Recognizing and understanding your feelings is an important part of knowing who you are, what you like and don't like, and what you want and don't want. When you know what you are feeling, it is easier to act assertively.

"I'm so confused," said Brian. "I feel all knotted up inside." "It sounds like you're having a lot of different feelings at once," said Margo, his counselor. Then she pointed to an aquarium on the wall behind her desk. "See how many different kinds of fish there are? Many colors, patterns, shapes, and sizes." "There are too many to see all at once," said Brian. "Yes," said Margo, "just like your feelings. But once you look closely and get to know them better, they don't seem so confusing."

"Let's look at these feelings fish," she said, putting a brightly colored piece of paper in front of Brian. The paper had pictures of many different fish, each with a different feeling word written inside. "Read through the words written on their bodies and see if you can find names for what you are feeling inside," said Margo. Brian did as she suggested and then pointed to four different fish. They were labeled "angry," "sad," "happy," and "nervous." "Good," said Margo. "Now tell me about your feelings."

"I'm thinking about the end of the school year," said Brian. "I feel angry because I am getting one low grade on my report card. I feel sad because when school is out I won't see my friends as much. I feel happy because I am going to camp. And I feel nervous because next year will be a new grade and I don't know what it will be like."

"Great job," said Margo. "Do you still feel confused?" "No," said Brian. "Now I know that I feel four separate things that were just tangled up inside me."

For You to Do

Color each feeling fish with a different color or pattern. When you are done, circle the fish that show five feelings you have felt in the last week. Then write a sentence about why you felt or are feeling that way.

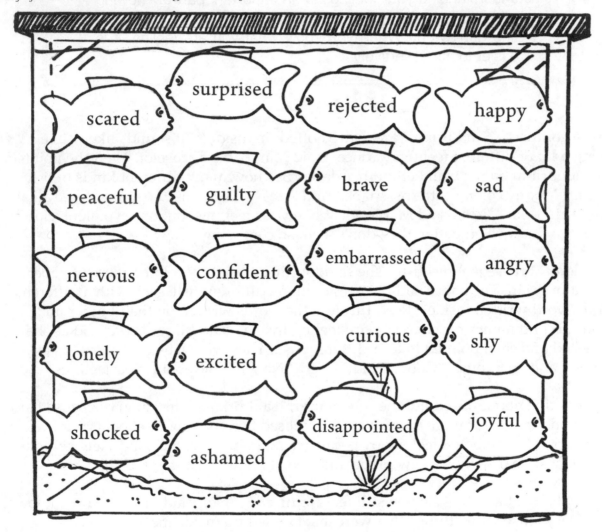

_____

_____

_____

... And More to Do

Write the names of five feelings that you like feeling the best.

1. _____
2. _____
3. _____
4. _____
5. _____

Write the names of five feelings that you like feeling the least.

1. _____
2. _____
3. _____
4. _____
5. _____

Write the names of any feelings whose meanings you don't understand. Then look in a dictionary or ask an adult for the definition, and write it next to the feeling. Make sure to use words that make sense to you.

_____

_____

_____

Activity 17   Managing Your Feelings

Mrs. Johnson, the school social worker, was talking to Jacob's class. "Who can tell me a feeling they've had today?" she asked.

"Happy!" said Jacob.

"Anyone else?" The students called out five more feelings: excited, lonely, bored, disappointed, and frustrated.

"Good job," said Mrs. Johnson. "You have just completed step one in managing your feelings, which is to *name them*." She pointed to a four-step plan she had written on a flip chart.

How to Manage Your Feelings

1. Name them.

2. Accept them.

3. Express them safely.

4. Decide what you need to take care of yourself.

"Step two," she said, "is to *accept your feelings*. You have a right to feel all feelings. If you ever feel excited, lonely, bored, disappointed, frustrated, or anything else, that's okay."

"The third step," she went on, "is to *express your feelings* so they don't bottle up inside of you and give you a headache or stomachache. But you have to let them out in a safe way. What's a safe way to let out sadness?"

"Talk to someone," said Jacob.

"Cry," said another student.

"Good!" said Mrs. Johnson. "What's an unsafe way to let out sadness?"

"Do something that would hurt you," someone said.

"Right again," said Mrs. Johnson, and she continued.

"Step four is to *decide what you need to take care of yourself.* We can either meet our needs by ourselves or ask for help. If you are feeling sad, how can you take care of yourself?"

"Try to fix whatever you're sad about," said one child.

"Right," said Mrs. Johnson, "and how could you ask for help?"

"Ask your mom for a hug," Jacob said.

"Good idea," said Mrs. Johnson. "You've learned the four steps. Remember, you can apply these steps to other feelings, too."

For You to Do

Pick a feeling by closing your eyes and pointing your finger anywhere on the circle. Open your eyes and see which feeling you have picked. Then fill in the chart. Repeat the game until you've used all the feelings.

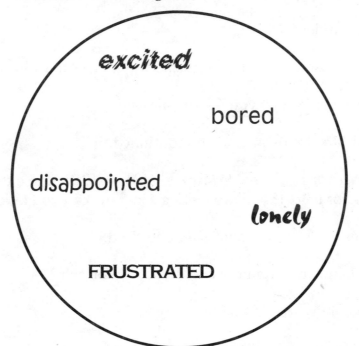

Name of Feeling	A Safe Way to Express This Feeling	How to Take Care of Myself

Copy this sentence on the next line: It's okay to feel all my feelings.

_____

... And More to Do

What feelings can you think of that are hard to name?

_____

_____

What feelings can you think of that are hard to accept?

_____

_____

What feelings can you think of that are hard to express safely?

_____

_____

What feelings make it hardest for you to take care of yourself?

_____

_____

Name three people who you could turn to when you need help managing your feelings.

_____

_____

_____

Describe a time when you saw someone manage a feeling well. Write the person's name, the feeling, and what that person did.

_____

_____

_____

Describe a time when you saw someone manage a feeling poorly. Write the person's name, the feeling, and what that person did.

_____

_____

_____

For You to Know

Learning to stay calm is one of the most important things you can do to manage your feelings and take care of yourself in a healthy way. Feeling peaceful inside can help you act assertively, standing up for yourself and respecting the rights of other people as well.

Grace seemed to get upset about everything. She became upset at small things, like when a button fell off her jeans or when her dog didn't want to sit on her lap. She became even more upset at big things: when her dog was missing for two days and when her mom had to go to the hospital.

Grace's parents were concerned. It seemed normal to become upset about the bigger things, but Grace became upset about *everything*. They tried to tell her to calm down, but Grace didn't seem to be able to. Then she got more upset because she couldn't calm down.

Finally her mother made an appointment for Grace at an anxiety clinic, a place where counselors helped people learn how to become calm and stay calm. The counselor told Grace that there were many things she could do to help herself feel more peaceful inside. There were things she could do for prevention—to keep her more calm every day no matter what happened. And there were things she could do for intervention—to help her calm down when something upsetting happened. He told her that many other people who became upset easily had been helped by learning these relaxation techniques, too. Grace felt a little better just knowing that.

Over the next few months, Grace went to the anxiety clinic two times a week. She learned how to do three helpful things when she started to feel upset:

1. Take deep, relaxing breaths.

2. Focus her mind on something peaceful instead of something stressful.

3. Change her thinking to help herself calm down.

Grace also learned to spend fifteen minutes each day practicing a calming activity. As Grace practiced these techniques, she started becoming less and less upset about little things. And when big things happened, she handled them better.

A Workbook to Help Kids Learn Assertiveness Skills

For You to Do

In the box on the left, draw a picture of Grace getting upset because she dropped her ice cream cone. Then choose one of the techniques she learned at the anxiety clinic. In the box on the right, draw a picture of Grace calming herself down by using that technique.

... And More to Do

You can try the same relaxation exercises that helped Grace. Try each of the exercises below and see how they feel for you. If you practice them every day, you will be able to stay calmer on a daily basis, even if nothing big is happening. If you practice them regularly, they will also come to you more easily when there is something big happening.

Take Deep, Relaxing Breaths

Before you try this exercise, notice how tense or stressed you are. Rate your tension on the scale below. Write "A" on the scale to show how much stress you are feeling.

1	2	3	4	5	6	7	8	9	10

Completely peaceful   Completely tense

Sit quietly and comfortably and close your eyes. Notice where your breath is. Is it moving in and out of your nose or your mouth? Is it moving down into your throat or your lungs? Follow its path for a minute or two. Now try to bring your breath down a little farther into your body. As you inhale, bring your breath all the way into your lungs and then deeper into your diaphragm, which is below your lungs. When you exhale, pay attention to letting all the air flow out of your body. Don't force it or become tense; just gently try to breathe more deeply. As you do this, your breath will automatically become slower. Practice these relaxing breaths for a few minutes.

When you are done, notice how tense you are now. Go back to the scale and rate your tension level again. This time, write "B" on the scale to show how much stress you are feeling.

Describe what it was like for you to do this exercise.

_____

_____

If your tension level changed from your first reading to your second, tell why you think that happened.

_____

_____

Focus on Something Peaceful

Think about something that has upset you lately or that is upsetting you right now. Close your eyes and think hard about how much that situation bothers you. Notice how tense you feel, and write "A" on the scale to show how much stress you are feeling.

1	2	3	4	5	6	7	8	9	10

Completely peaceful   Completely tense

Now close your eyes again and this time think of something that is very peaceful or pleasant, something that calms you. It might be something pretty in nature or a peaceful activity that you do. Picture it in your mind and pay attention to it for a few minutes.

When you are done, notice how tense you are now. Go back to the scale and this time, write "B" on the scale to show how much stress you are feeling.

Describe what it was like for you to do this exercise.

_____

_____

If your tension level changed from your first reading to your second, tell why you think that happened.

_____

_____

Change Your Thinking

Think about something that has upset you lately or that is upsetting you right now. Close your eyes and think of all the negative things about that situation. Focus on everything that you don't like about it or that you think is wrong. Spend a minute or two thinking about these negatives, and notice how tense you feel. Write "A" on the scale to show how much stress you are feeling.

1	2	3	4	5	6	7	8	9	10

Completely peaceful   Completely tense

Now close your eyes again, and this time change your thinking to focus on all the positive things about that situation. Think about anything at all that is good, that you like, or that you think is right. Spend a minute or two just focusing on and being happy about these positives.

When you are done, notice how tense you are. Go back to the scale and write "B" on the scale to show how much stress you are feeling.

Describe what it was like for you to do this exercise.

_____

_____

If your tension level changed from your first reading to your second, tell why you think that happened.

_____

_____

Think of a time of day that you could realistically spend fifteen minutes practicing these exercises or doing a calming activity. If this is hard to figure out, ask your parent or another grown-up to help you. Write the time that you think is best.

_____

The next time you become upset about something, try using one of these relaxation exercises to help you calm down.

For You to Know

Trying to speak or act when you are angry can be very difficult. Angry feelings usually make it hard for you to breathe deeply, think clearly, and make smart decisions. It is important to learn how to manage anger in a healthy way so that you can act assertively.

Owen had told his little brother Joseph over and over to leave his model cars alone and to play with them only when Owen was there. Now, for the third time, Joseph had broken one. Owen stormed out of his room. "Joseph!" he shouted at the top of his lungs.

Owen's mother came to see what was wrong. "Owen," she said, "you look like you're going to explode. Come here and sit down."

"I don't want to!" shouted Owen. "I want to smash all of Joseph's toys like he smashes mine!"

"Stop right now and take a deep breath," his mother said. Owen didn't want to listen to his mother, but he knew she was right. He sat down and took a slow, deep breath, and then another, and another. He finally started to feel the angry energy leave him. "Tell me what happened," his mother said. As Owen told her, he felt the anger returning. When his mother saw his anger rising again, she said, "Go outside and shoot some baskets. Don't come in until your anger is gone. Then we'll talk about what happened."

Owen went out with his basketball. The cold air felt good. He shot basket after basket, missing a lot of them, but he didn't care. After a while, he no longer felt angry. He went back inside and found his mother. "Now that you've gotten your anger out in a safe way, we can talk about what to do," she said. "You have the right to stand up for yourself, but you have to remember your brother's rights, too. You couldn't have thought clearly about either of those things until you let out your anger safely."

For You to Do

The phrases below describe ways to let out anger. Put a smiling face next to the ways that are safe. Put a frowning face next to the ways that are unsafe.

hitting an animal	writing graffiti on a wall
running into a busy street	counting to ten
taking deep breaths	shouting at another person
writing or drawing about how you feel	dancing fast
hitting a pillow	hitting a person
throwing a ball inside	jumping outside
running in the gym	jumping on your couch
stomping on a book	throwing a ball outside
holding your breath	spitting on someone
saying "I am angry"	riding your bike fast

... *And More to Do*

A basketball court is a good place to let out anger safely but it is not the only place. Tell how you could safely let out anger in each of the places below. Try to think of four activities for each place.

Your backyard

1. _____
2. _____
3. _____
4. _____

Your bedroom

1. _____
2. _____
3. _____
4. _____

Your basement

1. _____
2. _____
3. _____
4. _____

Cool, Calm, and Confident

An art room

1. _____

2. _____

3. _____

4. _____

Explain why you think it is important to let out anger safely instead of unsafely.

_____

_____

_____

For You to Know

When you choose friends who like you as you really are, you will feel good inside. When you choose friends who only like you when you try to be something they want, you will feel upset and confused. Having friends who like the real you will help you have the confidence to act assertively.

Nico felt stuck between two groups of kids at school. Part of him wanted to be friends with the very popular kids. When he was with them, he felt cool. Part of him wanted to be friends with a group of kids who were nice, but not as popular. When he was with them, he felt comfortable and relaxed, and he had a lot of fun. Every day he went back and forth in his mind: Who should he eat lunch with? If he sat with the popular kids, he would tell jokes that he didn't really like but that those kids thought were funny. They would laugh and tell him he was cool, and then he would feel cool. He would also talk about baseball. He really didn't like baseball, but those kids did, so he would join in their conversation and pretend to like it. Then they would think he was cool, and he would think so, too.

If he ate lunch with the kids who weren't as popular, he would tell jokes that he really liked, and even some he made up himself. They would laugh with him and his laughter would be real. They would talk about soccer. Nico loved soccer, and so did these kids. If he ate lunch with them, he knew he would have a lot of fun, but he wouldn't feel quite as cool.

Nico wasn't sure what to do. As he stood with his lunch tray, looking from one group's table to the other's, Mr. Adams, the custodian, came up to him. "Looks like you're in a predicament," said Mr. Adams.

"I sure am," said Nico, and he told Mr. Adams about his problem.

"Well," said Mr. Adams, "it sounds like when you're with the more popular kids you feel cool on the surface, but how do you feel about yourself inside?"

Nico thought for a minute. "Not good at all," he said.

"Why?" asked Mr. Adams.

"Because," explained Nico, "I know those kids only like me because I pretend to be like them. If I were the real me, they wouldn't like me."

"Interesting," said Mr. Adams. "And how do you feel inside when you're with the other group?"

"Great," said Nico, "both inside and on the surface. I feel good because they know the real me and they like that person. I don't have to pretend."

"Sounds like you've got your problem licked," said Mr. Adams. "Just decide if you want to feel good about yourself on the surface or deep down inside. Decide if you want to choose friends who like the real you or the pretend you. Good luck, Nico!"

For You to Do

Tell who you think Nico chose to eat lunch with, and why.

_____

_____

Do you ever pretend to be someone you're not to get other people to like you? In the first box, draw what you look like when you are the real you. Show what clothes you wear, how your face and hair look, and what you say. Answer the questions on the right about who you really are. Below the picture, write the names of the people who are your friends when you are the real you.

The Real Me	What is your favorite sport?

What is your favorite sport?

_____

What do you like to do on Saturdays?

_____

Do you like to read?

_____

What is your favorite restaurant?

_____

What do you like to do after school?

_____

Is getting good grades important to you?

_____

_____   _____

_____   _____

_____   _____

Choosing Real Friends

Activity 20

In the second box, draw what you look like when you are the pretend you. Show what clothes you wear, how your face and hair look, and what you say. Answer the questions on the right about who you are pretending to be. Below the picture, write the names of the people who are your friends when you are the pretend you.

The Pretend Me

What is your favorite sport?

_____

What do you like to do on Saturdays?

_____

Do you like to read?

_____

What is your favorite restaurant?

_____

What do you like to do after school?

_____

Is getting good grades important to you?

_____

_____   _____

_____   _____

_____   _____

... And More to Do

Tell how you feel inside when you are the real you.

_____

_____

_____

Tell how you feel inside when you are the pretend you.

_____

_____

_____

Tell why you sometimes want to be something you're not.

_____

_____

_____

Make a list of the friends that like you for who you really are.

_____

_____

_____

Tell how you feel when you are with these friends.

_____

_____

_____

Make a list of friends you have chosen who are being true to themselves.

_____

_____

_____

Make a list of friends you have chosen who are pretending to be something they're really not.

_____

_____

_____

Which of the above two groups of friends do you feel best about spending time with, and why?

_____

_____

_____

Activity 21

Taking Responsibility for Your Actions

For You to Know

You have a choice in every action you take. Taking responsibility for your actions means that you admit to the actions that have good outcomes and also those that have poor outcomes. When your choices do turn out well, you can celebrate. When they don't, you can learn from your mistakes. Taking responsibility for your choices and actions can build your confidence and help you act assertively.

Mrs. Grayman had seen Madeline and Ria talking during a test and asked them to stay after class. Madeline didn't want to get into trouble and didn't want her parents to know. When Mrs. Grayman asked, she denied talking; she didn't want to tell the truth for fear of getting punished.

Ria also didn't want to get into trouble and didn't want her parents to know. But when Mrs. Grayman questioned her, she admitted talking to Madeline. Ria said that she knew she shouldn't have done it, that she was sorry, and it wouldn't happen again. Ria was afraid she would be punished, but she knew she would get in worse trouble if she lied.

Mrs. Grayman told the girls that their stories were different, but that she had seen them talking and even heard one of their classmates telling them to be quiet. She said she would call their parents and they would have to stay after school on Friday.

Madeline's parents said she was wrong to disobey the rules and also wrong to lie. They said she needed to learn to take responsibility for her actions; she would have to write a note of apology to Mrs. Grayman and also to Ria. And when she got home from school on Friday, she would stay in for the evening and help with cleaning chores. Madeline pouted and said she shouldn't have to do any of this because it was Ria's fault, not hers.

Ria's parents also said she was wrong to disobey the rules, but she was right to tell the truth. They said that staying after school would be enough to make up for her mistake. Ria said she knew she'd been wrong and wouldn't do it again, and she meant it.

Cool, Calm, and Confident

For You to Do

A group of children were playing ball in the house and broke a vase. Some of them made statements that sounded like they were taking responsibility for their actions. Color these conversation balloons green. Some of them made statements that sounded like they were not taking responsibility for their actions. Color these conversation balloons red.

What do you think the parents whose house it is will do about the children who are taking responsibility?

_____

_____

What do you think the parents whose house it is will do about the children who are not taking responsibility?

_____

_____

... And More to Do

Think about a time you did something wrong and did not take responsibility or tried to blame someone else for your actions. Describe it here.

_____

_____

What were you afraid might happen if you took responsibility for your actions?

_____

_____

Tell how you felt about yourself inside after you blamed another person.

_____

_____

Imagine you had taken responsibility for your actions. What might have happened differently?

_____

_____

Tell how you would have felt inside if you had taken this action instead of the first.

_____

_____

Taking Responsibility
for Your Actions

Describe a time when someone blamed you for something you did not do.

_____

_____

Tell how you felt when this happened.

_____

_____

Tell why it might sometimes feel hard or scary to take responsibility for your actions.

_____

_____

For You to Know

Part of acting assertively and standing up for yourself means using your right to say no. You have the right to let other people know when you do not want to do or say something that would hurt you or that you do not think is right. Learning and practicing different ways to say no can make it easier to act assertively when you want to.

Officer Carlson was visiting Christopher's school. She was talking to the kids about the importance of resisting drugs, alcohol, cigarettes, and anything else that could hurt them or get them in trouble. "What else should you learn how to say no to?" she asked the class.

"Cheating," said one student. "Lying," said another. "Stealing," said another.

"Good," said Officer Carlson. "You get the idea. Now think about someone you really like coming up to you and offering you a cigarette. Maybe this is a person you have wanted to be friends with for a long time. Maybe it is a very popular kid, and you feel pressure to say yes. You know smoking will hurt you, but you really want this kid to like you. What do you do?"

The class was quiet. "Sometimes it's really hard to say no," said Christopher. "That's right," said Officer Carlson. "Sometimes it is. That's why it's important to think about it and practice it *before* you are in that position so you can do it even when you are feeling shy. Saying no is an important way to assert yourself, protect yourself, and stand up for your rights. Today I'm going to teach you a few ways to say no, and you can practice them together."

Officer Carlson divided the class into groups and wrote these ideas on the chalkboard:

1. Use the word "no."

2. Name the behavior and say that you don't do that.

3. Give reasons for saying no.

4. Suggest doing something else instead.

In their groups, the students came up with ways to follow these directions. Here is what they decided:

1. Ways to use the word "no": "No." "No thanks." "No thanks, I don't want to." "No, I don't want to smoke." "No, you can't have my lunch money."

2. Ways to name the behavior and say you don't do that: "That's cheating; I don't do that." "That's against the rules; I'm not going to do that." "That's a drug that could hurt me; I won't do that."

3. Reasons for saying no: "No, I'm not going to do that; I could get hurt." "No, I won't smoke; I could get cancer." "No, I don't want to lie; it would make me feel bad about myself."

4. Ways to suggest doing something else: "No, I don't want to drink. Why don't we ride bikes instead?" "No, I don't want to break into that kid's locker, but I'll play a game with you." "No, I don't want to do that. If you want to do something else, let me know."

Christopher and his classmates practiced the many ways of saying no out loud until they were comfortable with them and the words came naturally and easily.

"How do you feel about saying no now?" asked Officer Carlson when they were done. "I feel good," said Christopher. "I know I have the right to stand up for myself when I don't want to do something, no matter who is asking me."

For You to Do

The children in these pictures are being asked to do something they don't want to do. Help each child say no by choosing a statement from the group on the next page and writing it on the lines beneath the picture. More than one statement may fit each picture; choose the one you think fits best.

... *And More to Do*

Put your initials next to any of these statements that you would be comfortable using to refuse something you don't want to do.

_____ No.

_____ No, thanks.

_____ No, I don't want to.

_____ No, I'd rather not.

_____ No, I don't think that's a good idea.

_____ No, thanks. I don't do that

_____ No, I don't want any of that.

_____ No, I don't believe in doing that.

_____ No way. That's not a smart idea.

_____ No, I don't want to get into trouble or get hurt.

_____ No, I respect myself too much to do that.

Find a grown-up to role-play with you. Ask the grown-up to ask you the questions below, and use one of your refusal statements to answer.

Will you take that girl's purse when she leaves her seat? I'll be your friend if you do it.

We're going to try these drugs. Want to have some fun with us?

Why won't you try it? Are you chicken?

Come on, just drink some. Don't you want to be cool?

Describe a situation where it is hard for you to say no even though you want to.

_____

_____

Talk to a grown-up about how you can make it easier to stand up for yourself. Tell what you can do to feel stronger.

_____

_____

> ## *For You to Know*
>
> Human beings have certain rights just because they are alive. That includes you. When you know and understand these rights, you can feel more confident in standing up for yourself when you need to. Knowing your rights can help you to act assertively, respecting your own rights and the rights of others as well.

Just because you exist, you have the right to:

- Be cared for and protected by an adult, such as a parent or guardian. If there is not an adult in your life who is providing you with food, clothing, shelter, education, and health care, you have the right to ask for the help you need.

- Be treated with respect, and not hurt, physically or emotionally. Other people of all ages should treat you kindly and respect both your feelings and your body.

- Say no without feeling guilty or selfish if someone asks you to do something illegal or immoral, something that your heart tells you is not right or that would get you in trouble.

If someone ever ignores your rights or tries to take them away, you have the right to stand up for yourself in an appropriate manner. It is important that you choose a way of standing up for your rights that does not hurt anyone else or ignore their rights. If you are not respecting the rights of others, then you are doing the same thing to them that they are doing to you.

You have the right to stand up for yourself with children your age, with older kids, and even with adults. You have the right to protect your rights with people you know and with strangers. You have the right to act assertively in any situation.

You can stand up for your rights by the way you speak and the way you act. You can tell someone that they are violating your rights by what they are doing, and you can act to protect your rights.

For You to Do

Color the downward-pointing arrow next to each situation that would violate your rights. Color the upward-pointing arrow next to each situation that would not violate your rights. Some of the answers may not be clear at first. If you are unsure of an answer, share your thoughts with an adult before making your decision.

⇧ ⇩ Your mother said you couldn't have dessert because you didn't eat your vegetables.

⇧ ⇩ A classmate asked if you could help her understand the homework assignment.

⇧ ⇩ An older student in your school told you that you had to smoke a cigarette or he would take your backpack.

⇧ ⇩ Your father asked you to clean your room.

⇧ ⇩ Your mother refused to feed you because she was mad at you.

⇧ ⇩ An older student in your school poured glue in your shoes.

⇧ ⇩ A teacher asked you to help her straighten the desks in the classroom.

⇧ ⇩ A classmate stole your homework, then put his name on it and turned it in.

⇧ ⇩ A friend asked you to lie to her parents about where she had been.

⇧ ⇩ You broke your arm when you fell off your bike. Your stepfather said he wouldn't take you to the doctor because you hadn't asked for permission to ride your bike that day.

⇧ ⇩ A friend asked to borrow your markers.

⇧ ⇩ Another student said he would not let you onto the school bus unless you gave him your lunch money.

Cool, Calm, and Confident

... And More to Do

Describe a time when it is easy for you to stand up for your rights.

_____

_____

_____

Describe a time when it is hard for you to stand up for your rights.

_____

_____

_____

Describe anything that has happened to you recently where you felt that your rights were violated.

_____

_____

_____

Tell a grown-up about what happened and talk about the best way to stand up for your rights if this situation happens again. Draw a picture of yourself standing up for your rights in this situation. On the lines below your picture, write the words you would use to stand up for yourself.

_____

_____

_____

"I Feel" Statements

> ## *For You to Know*
>
> One way to communicate assertively is by using "I feel" statements. Beginning a statement with the words "I feel" shows that you are standing up for yourself and that you are taking responsibility for your feelings. When you use "I feel" statements, other people are less likely to feel judged, attacked, or criticized.

Molly felt left out of the lunchtime conversation because her friends were talking together with their chairs turned away from her. She tried to join in but no one was listening to her. She felt very frustrated and wanted to say, "You are so rude. I hate you all!" Instead, she tapped one friend on the shoulder and said, "I feel lonely when you turn away from me and exclude me from the conversation because I want to join in, too." The kids said they were sorry; they didn't realize she was being left out. Then they turned their chairs and made room for Molly to join them.

Michael's older brother said, "Hi, Shorty," and patted Michael on the head like he always did. Michael felt embarrassed that he was shorter and hated when his brother called him that name. Michael started to say, "Get away from me. I wish you were someone else's brother!" Instead, he said, "I feel hurt when you call me Shorty because I don't like being the shortest one." His brother stopped what he was doing and told Michael that he had never realized the nickname was hurtful. He apologized and said he wouldn't call Michael Shorty anymore.

Colin didn't realize his shoelace was untied, and he tripped when he was walking down the hallway at school. He fell flat on his face, and a boy who was watching started laughing at him. Colin wanted to get up and kick the boy hard in the shin, but he knew that wasn't the right thing to do. Instead, he said, "I feel embarrassed and angry when you laugh at me. Falling like that was just a mistake that could have happened to anyone. I'd like you to stop laughing now." The boy was surprised at how Colin stood up for himself, and he stopped laughing.

Cassie got a bad grade on her science report. She went up to the teacher's desk and was going to tell her, "You are an unfair grader. I hate this class!" Instead, she said, "I felt disappointed when I got this grade because I worked hard on this report and I thought I'd do better." The teacher said she could look over the report with Cassie after school, and maybe they would find a way to bring the grade up.

Antonio felt very upset when the other kids wouldn't let him shoot baskets with them because he wasn't very good at it. Antonio wanted to grab their ball and run away with it or throw it up in a tree. Instead he said, "I feel sad and frustrated when you won't let me play with you because I'll never get better if I don't have a chance to practice." The other kids thought about that for a minute and realized that Antonio was right. They threw him the ball and told him to give it a try.

"I Feel" Statements

Activity 24

For You to Do

What do you think would have happened if Molly had actually said, "You are so rude. I hate you all!" to her friends?

_____

_____

_____

What do you think would have happened if Michael had actually said, "Get away from me. I wish you were someone else's brother!" to his brother?

_____

_____

_____

What do you think would have happened if Colin had actually kicked the boy who laughed at him?

_____

_____

_____

What do you think would have happened if Cassie had actually said, "You are an unfair grader. I hate this class!" to her teacher?

_____

_____

_____

A Workbook to Help Kids Learn Assertiveness Skills

101

What do you think would have happened if Antonio had actually grabbed the boys' basketball?

_____

_____

_____

Number the names of the kids from 1 to 5 in order of who you think had the hardest time using an "I feel" statement. Then tell why.

_____ Molly

_____ Michael

_____ Colin

_____ Cassie

_____ Antonio

_____

_____

_____

"I Feel" Statements

... And More to Do

Read the statements below and think about what the speaker might be feeling. Then rewrite each statement to turn it into an "I feel" statement.

"You're a creep. You lied to me."

I feel _____

when _____

because _____.

"I don't want to do the dishes again. I hate you, Mom."

I feel _____

when _____

because _____.

"Band is stupid. I made one little mistake, and the band director yelled at me."

I feel _____

when _____

because _____.

A Workbook to Help Kids Learn Assertiveness Skills

103

"You made me bat last. You're the worst team captain I ever had, and I hope I'm never on your team again."

I feel _____

when _____

because _____.

"I hate swimming with you. All you ever do is splash me and dunk me."

I feel _____

when _____

because _____.

Describe something that happened to you recently where you could have used an "I feel" statement to speak assertively. Then write the "I feel" statement you could have used.

_____

_____

_____

I feel _____

when _____

because _____.

For You to Know

Being assertive includes knowing how to make polite conversation with other people. It can feel a little scary to talk to people when you think you don't know what to say, but a few simple guidelines can help you. When you follow these guidelines, it will be easier for you to make conversation.

If you would like to talk to someone, you can start by asking them a question. The letter "W" can help you remember five question words to start conversations. For example, Sheena is sitting next to Abby and would like to be friends with her but doesn't know what to talk about. Then she remembers the five Ws and thinks of these questions to ask Abby:

Who is your favorite singer?

What are you doing after school?

When are you getting your braces off?

Where do you live?

Why do you think the teacher gave us so much homework today?

When Sheena asked Abby a question, Abby answered it, and a conversation started. Sheena listened to Abby's answer and then talked about what Abby had said. When Sheena ran out of things to say, she asked Abby another question. She learned a lot about Abby and took steps toward making a new friend. Abby felt happy that Sheena was interested in her and her thoughts and feelings.

For You to Do

Draw a large W in the first box. Next to the W, write the question words: Who, What, When, Where, and Why. Write each question word in a different color.

In the second box, draw a picture of yourself and someone you would like to talk to. On the lines below it, write five questions you could ask this person. Begin each question with a different one of the five Ws.

_____

_____

_____

_____

... And More to Do

Fill in the blank spaces with the W word that would fit best in the question. Then write the name of a person you might ask the question.

_____ is your name? _____

_____ do you get up in the morning?_____

_____ does your grandmother live?_____

_____ are you wearing a swimsuit?_____

_____ is going to be your partner?_____

_____ would you like to dance with?_____

_____ is your favorite place to go on vacation?_____

_____ will you be old enough to drive?_____

_____ do you want to do on Saturday?_____

_____ aren't you going to the park with us?_____

Think of a W question you could ask each of the following people, and write the question on the blank lines.

Person who lives in a tree house: _____

Sailor: _____

Firefighter: _____

Abraham Lincoln: _____

Smartest person in the world: _____

Newborn baby: _____

Oldest person in the world: _____

Alien: _____

Astronaut: _____

President of the United States: _____

Can you list the five W words from memory? Without looking back in the text, write as many as you can remember here.

_____

_____

Accepting and Giving Compliments

For You to Know

Accepting and giving compliments in a kind manner is part of feeling good about yourself. When you can both accept compliments and give them sincerely, you are acting assertively.

When Cody's scoutmaster told the troop that Cody was going to win an award, Cody started to jump around, saying, "I'm the greatest, I'm the greatest!" When Cody's teacher told him he'd done a great job on his oral report, Cody said, "I messed up when I was talking—three times."

Cody's dad noticed that Cody didn't handle compliments well and said, "You are a good person, and you do many things well. You have to start believing in yourself and accepting the praise people give you. When people compliment you, tell yourself they are being honest; you have done something good. Then look them in the eye and say thank you." Cody wasn't sure he could do that, but he promised his dad he would try.

The next time Cody's aunt told him he had such a bright smile, Cody started making fun of it, saying, "I'm a light bulb!" But then he stopped, looked at her, and said, "Thanks, Aunt Lynda." Afterward, Cody felt better about himself. He finally started believing the truth: there were many good things about him to be proud of.

"You can give compliments, too," his dad explained further. "You can tell people when you really appreciate something they have done or said, or when you recognize that they do something well. Look for a chance to do that today."

That afternoon Cody was skateboarding with his friend Ryan. "You're really good on the ramps," Cody told him.

Ryan's face lit up. "Thanks," he said. "I've been practicing a lot." Cody realized that he felt good inside when he complimented Ryan. It made him feel more strong and confident about himself as well.

For You to Do

The kids in the situations below are all receiving compliments. You can tell how they feel about themselves inside by the way they respond. If you think these children feel good about themselves inside, write G in their shirts. If you think they feel bad about themselves inside, write B in their shirts. Explain your answer under the situation.

When Miguel's teacher gave back a story he had written, she said, "You're a good writer, Miguel. You deserve this A." Miguel smiled and said, "Thank you."

_____

_____

When Miguel's teacher gave back a story he had written, she said, "You're a good writer, Miguel. You deserve this A." Miguel made a face and said, "Yeah, I'm so good, they're interviewing me on TV tonight!"

_____

_____

When Leah sang a new song she had just learned, her mother said, "You have a beautiful voice, Leah." Leah smiled and said, "Thanks, Mom."

_____

_____

When Leah sang a new song she had just learned, her mother said, "You have a beautiful voice, Leah." Leah bit her lip and said, "I can never hit the high notes, and I forget the words."

_____

_____

Liza hugged Claire and said, "You're a great friend!" Claire smiled and said, "Thanks!"

_____

_____

Liza hugged Claire and said, "You're a great friend!" Claire said sarcastically, "Yeah, I'm so popular, you should be glad I even talk to you!"

_____

_____

... And More to Do

In the frame below, draw or paste a picture of something you do well that another person could sincerely compliment you about. Underneath the picture, write a compliment someone might give you and what you would say in response.

A compliment to me: _____

_____

My response: _____

_____

Draw a picture of three different people you know and write their names in the frames below. Next to each picture, write one sincere compliment you can give that person. It is important to be truthful when giving a compliment; don't say it unless you really mean it.

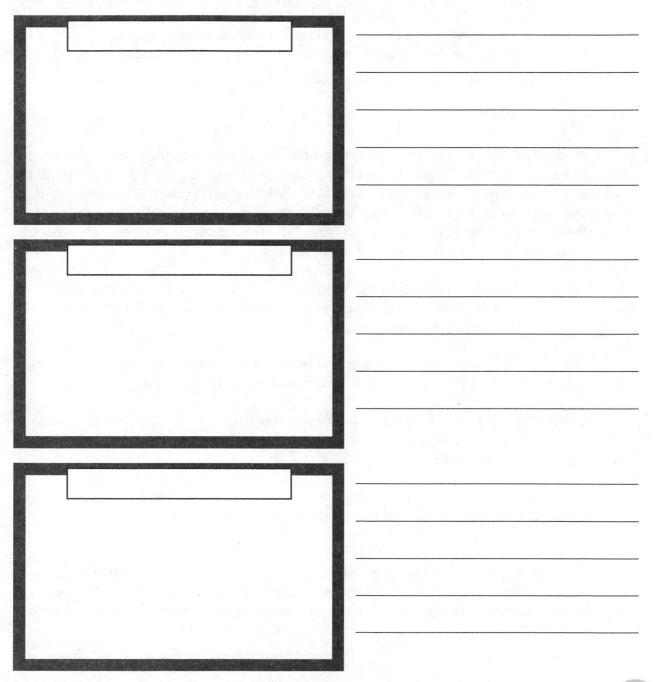

Activity 27

Assertiveness with a Group

For You to Know

Approaching a new group of kids may feel a little scary at first. You may not know what to say or do to join in with them, but you can learn how to act assertively in this situation, standing up for yourself and respecting the rights of others as well.

Every week Ms. Klowacki met with a group of kids to help them learn about how to make and keep friends. "I want to join Boy Scouts," said Jared, "but I'm afraid to go to the first meeting where everyone else will already know each other." "I want to make new friends at school," said Elise, "but I don't know how to start." "I want to play at the park in my neighborhood," said Juan, "but I'm afraid to approach the kids who are already playing there. What if they are mean to me?"

Ms. Klowacki said it was normal to feel worried about approaching a new group, but there were things they could do to make it easier and more likely that a group would accept them. Here is what she suggested:

1. Wait for a lull in the conversation or a break in the game. It's rude to start talking over someone else or to break in to a game that's already going on.

2. Check out the faces of all the kids. Who is wearing the friendliest smile? Who might you have something in common with? Approach someone who looks likely to talk to a new person.

3. Smile, and when the time is right, approach the friendliest-looking person. Use a polite, friendly greeting that feels right for you. "May I join you?" or "Hi, do you have room for one more?" are two examples.

4. Go with the flow of what's already happening. If the kids are talking about school, talk about school. If the group is playing soccer, play soccer. You will fit in more easily if you go with what they are doing at first, rather than trying to change them.

For You to Do

The pictures below show Jared, Elise, and Juan in situations where they want to join in a new group. In each picture, circle the child who looks the friendliest and should be approached first. Write when you think Jared, Elise, and Juan should join in, what friendly greetings they could use, and what they should do or talk about at first.

_____

_____

_____

_____

_____

_____

_____

_____

_____

_____

_____

_____

_____

_____

_____

_____

_____

... And More to Do

On a separate piece of paper, write a short story about a child who tries to join a group but acts too passively and gets rejected.

Now rewrite the story. Tell how the child acts assertively by using Ms. Klowacki's guidelines and gets accepted by the group.

Next, write another story about a child who tries to join a group but acts too aggressively and gets rejected.

Describe how you could use Ms. Klowacki's guidelines to approach a group you would like to join.

_____

_____

_____

Tell which of the guidelines are easiest for you to use, and why.

_____

_____

_____

Tell which of the guidelines are hardest for you to use, and why.

_____

_____

_____

For You to Know

Adults have the job of making and enforcing rules for children to follow. When you are an adult, that will be your job, too. As a child, you may not be able to make the rules, but you can express your opinion or ask a question about them if you act appropriately and assertively.

Olivia worked very hard all summer on improving her basket-shooting skills. She had practiced at home with her dad and at the park with her friends. Her older brother had helped her, too. Olivia thought she was making more baskets than ever, even if she might not be as good as the best kids on the team. When the new season opened, the coach placed her on second string, which meant she might sit on the bench the whole season. Olivia felt hurt and angry. She wanted to yell at the coach, and she wanted to tell him he wasn't fair, but she knew that the coach made the rules.

Olivia's dad noticed how sad she looked that night at dinner, and he asked her what was wrong. Olivia explained what had happened, and her dad said that she had done the right thing. He told her that yelling aggressively at the coach wouldn't have been appropriate and wouldn't have helped her get a place on first string, but there was something she could do. "What's that?" asked Olivia.

"You can act assertively, standing up for your rights while respecting the rights of the coach at the same time."

"How do I do that?" Olivia asked.

"Well," her dad answered, "you need to think about how you can express your feelings and thoughts to the coach while still being respectful. You have the right to do that. You may not be able to change your place on the team, but you can stand up for yourself and tell him what you think." Olivia's dad suggested that she write down everything she was thinking and feeling, and then go back over it and pick out the things she wanted to tell the coach in words that would express her ideas but still be respectful. Here is what she wrote:

I feel so angry I could scream! I worked so hard all summer, practicing, practicing, practicing—even when I didn't feel like it. I want to play basketball so much! I feel so mad that the stupid coach didn't let me be on first string. I think he is a dummy! I think he is mean! I want to yell at him! I know that I shouldn't do those things so I won't. But I really want to!

What I want to tell the coach in a respectful way:

1. I practiced very hard to improve. I practiced alone, with my brother, and with other kids, almost every day, all summer.

2. I feel sad and disappointed that I was placed on second string, even though I have tried so hard to improve.

3. I think I have improved. Even if I'm not the most talented player, I have gotten a lot better since last year.

"Good job," said Olivia's dad. "Now, ask the coach politely when you can talk to him about this. When you talk to him, treat him with respect, just as you'd want him to do for you."

Olivia talked with the coach the next day after school. Quietly and calmly, she told him her thoughts. When she was through, the coach smiled and said, "Olivia, I'm very proud of you. You handled this in a very healthy and mature way. I am impressed by your hard work and also by the respectful way you talked to me. I am proud to have you on our team. I am still going to keep you on second string for the first few games, but if you keep practicing, I will let you try playing on first string once the season gets underway. If your skills continue to improve, I can tell that you will be a great asset to our team."

For You to Do

The lines below were written by children who were upset about things that adults had done. They expressed their feelings on paper because it wouldn't have been respectful to say them to the adults. Read what they have written and then, on the blank lines, tell how they could have expressed themselves assertively but respectfully.

I feel sad and mad and upset. My best friend Ginny's parents told her they are moving to another state. I hate them right now! They are taking away my best friend! I am going to miss her so much! What if I never get to see her again? They are the meanest parents I ever met!

_____

_____

_____

_____

_____

_____

That stupid Mrs. Jones! She is the meanest old lady there ever was! Yesterday I was riding my bike fast down the sidewalk and I accidentally ran over some of her roses and broke them. She yelled at me in front of all my friends. I felt so embarrassed. I didn't mean to break her flowers. It was an accident. Now I feel like breaking all her other roses, too.

_____

_____

_____

_____

_____

_____

I hate my math teacher. She gave me a bad grade again. This time I studied really hard for the test, but it was so hard I couldn't even understand all the instructions. I am so mad that I wish they would fire her! If she had let me ask a question during the test, maybe I could have done the problems right. She's not fair. I hate her rules.

_____

_____

_____

_____

_____

_____

... And More to Do

Think of a time when you were feeling upset because of something an adult did. Write your thoughts and feelings about what happened here.

_____

_____

_____

Underline the statements you wrote that would not be respectful or appropriate to express to the adult.

Write what you could have said to the adult about this situation that would have shown assertiveness: standing up for your rights, but respecting the rights of the adult as well.

_____

_____

_____

Describe a situation in your life now where you would like to express your thoughts and feelings assertively to an adult.

_____

_____

_____

Write your thoughts and feelings here.

_____

_____

_____

Write what you could say to the adult that would show assertiveness.

_____

_____

_____

For You to Know

We have a better chance of working out disagreements with other people when we try to handle them assertively rather than passively or aggressively. When you can see both yourself and the other person as separate from the problem you are dealing with, it is easier to work as a team. Then you can stand up for yourself and still respect the rights of the other person.

James and Mikayla were arguing. James thought the class should collect coats for needy people for their holiday project. Mikayla thought the class should collect canned goods. "Warm clothing is more important!" said James. "Food is more important!" said Mikayla.

Finally, the teacher, Mrs. Drew, told James and Mikayla that they weren't solving their problem by arguing. She asked them to sit across from each other. "Let's define the problem," she said. "The problem is James," said Mikayla. "The problem is Mikayla," said James. "Let's think more clearly," said Mrs. Drew. "The problem isn't James or Mikayla. You both have good ideas. The real problem is that you don't agree." Mrs. Drew wrote the problem on a piece of paper and set it on the table between them. "Now, we've separated the problem from the people. James and Mikayla, I want you to work as a team and figure out how to solve this problem."

At first James and Mikayla didn't know what to do. They were so used to arguing with each other, it felt unfamiliar to be on the same team. Finally they started talking. "Well," said James, "it's true that both of our ideas are good." "But neither of us wants to give ours up," said Mikayla. "Right," said James. "Do you think there's any way we could do both ideas?" "That would solve the problem," said Mikayla. "Maybe we could do a clothing *and* food drive," said James. "That's a good idea," said Mikayla. "Or maybe we could do a clothing drive now and a food drive in spring." "That's a good idea, too," said James. They looked at each other and smiled.

For You to Do

Use the outlines below to show James and Mikayla when they are arguing and saying that the other person is the problem. Show how they feel by drawing the looks on their faces. On the lines below each face, tell what they originally think is the problem.

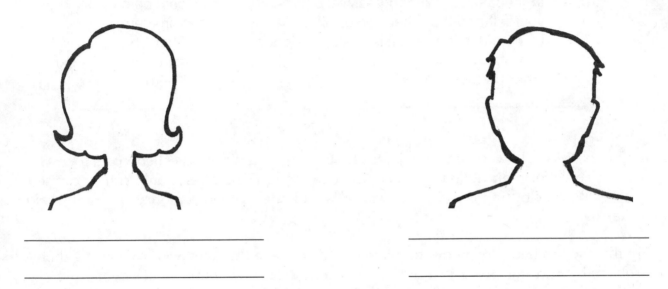

_____

_____

Now show James and Mikayla separating themselves from the problem and working as a team. On the lines below the table tell what the problem is when they put it outside of themselves. Show how they feel by drawing the looks on their faces.

_____

_____

How did James and Mikayla feel toward each other when each thought the other was the problem?

_____

_____

How did they feel toward each other when they put the problem outside themselves?

_____

_____

How much did James and Mikayla accomplish toward solving the problem when each thought the other was the problem?

_____

_____

How much did they accomplish toward solving the problem when they put it outside themselves?

_____

_____

Which do you think works better as a problem-solving method: thinking of the other person as the problem or seeing the problem as separate from each of you? Tell why.

_____

_____

... And More to Do

Describe a problem that you are having trouble working out with another person.

_____

_____

_____

Draw a picture of the two of you facing each other, and draw something that represents the problem between the two of you, but separate from each of you.

Describe how you could work as a team with this person to solve the problem now that it is separate from you both.

_____

_____

_____

For You to Know

Most of the time, we see experiences only through our own eyes. But when we try to see them through another person's eyes, we can better understand how that person feels, and solving problems becomes easier.

Lakiesha and Hailey were walking through the carnival's House of Fun. Each was wearing a special pair of glasses. Lakiesha's made everything look bigger. Hailey's made everything look smaller. "Wow, everything is huge!" said Lakiesha. "No, it's not," said Hailey. "Everything is tiny!" The girls laughed and then they traded glasses. "When I look though your glasses, everything looks different," said Lakiesha. "It's the same when I look through yours," said Hailey.

Later, the girls went to get ice cream. Lakiesha didn't like any of the flavors, while Hailey liked all of them. Lakiesha went home and told her family that the ice cream at the carnival wasn't any good. Hailey told her family that the ice cream at the carnival was wonderful. Lakiesha and Hailey saw things differently.

That night, Lakiesha told Hailey she'd had fun, but she didn't want to go to the carnival again. At first Hailey felt mad. "Why don't you want to go to the carnival with me again? Don't you want to be my friend?" she asked. "Yes, I want to be your friend," said Lakiesha. "But my feet hurt, I'm out of money, and my stomach is queasy from all those rides." "Oh," said Hailey, "I can see why you wouldn't want to go again for a while."

Lakiesha and Hailey were seeing the carnival through different eyes. This is what happens when two people look at one situation and think different things about it. When Hailey saw things only through her own eyes, she felt mad at Lakiesha. When Lakiesha explained how she felt, Hailey could see things through her friend's eyes. Then she understood why Lakiesha didn't want to go to the carnival again.

For You to Do

In each of these situations, one child is mad at the other. Decide which child needs to see things through the other's eyes. Then write what that child might say if he or she could see the other person's point of view.

Jake and Kevin are standing on a pier with a boat docked next to it. Jake is scared, and he thinks, "I don't want to go in the boat because I don't know how to swim." Kevin says, "I'm mad that you don't want to go for a boat ride! I was looking forward to it!"

Which child needs to see things through the other's eyes? Color the eyeglasses next to that child's name.

 Jake    Kevin

What might that child say if he could see the other's point of view?

_____

_____

Dana and Julie are looking at each other angrily with their arms crossed in front of them. Dana thinks, "I don't want Julie to come to my house because I'm embarrassed that it is so dirty." Julie says, "It's mean of you not to let me come over. I invite you to my house all the time."

Which child needs to see things through the other's eyes? Color the eyeglasses next to that child's name.

 Dana    Julie

What might that child say if she could see the other's point of view?

_____

_____

Seeing Another Person's Point of View

Lily is looking at Zoe meanly. Lily says, "I'm mad because you didn't come to my skating party." Zoe thinks, "I'm a terrible skater; I'd rather go to the library or a movie with Lily."

Which child needs to see things through the other's eyes? Color the eyeglasses next to that child's name.

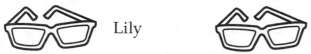

What might that child say if she could see the other's point of view?

_____

_____

Noah is mad at his dad. He says, "I don't want to wear a helmet when I ride my bike. You treat me like a baby!" His dad thinks, "I know a boy who was badly hurt when he fell off his bike. I love you so much; I don't want that to happen to you."

Which person needs to see things through the other's eyes? Color the eyeglasses next to that person's name.

What might that person say if he could see the other's point of view?

_____

_____

... *And More to Do*

How do you think seeing someone else's point of view could help you respect that person's feelings?

_____

_____

_____

How do you think seeing someone else's point of view could help you solve problems with that person?

_____

_____

_____

Write the name of someone who does not understand your point of view and so is mad at you. What would you like that person to understand?

_____

_____

Write the name of someone you are mad at whose point of view you might not understand. Try to imagine what it is like to be that person. Write what you think that person's point of view might be.

_____

_____

You can stand up for yourself by telling people your point of view in a nice way. You can respect other people's rights by trying to understand their point of view. Both of these actions are part of acting assertively.

Seeing Your Part in the Problem

For You to Know

It might feel easier to blame someone else for a problem, but solving a problem is easier when both people can see their parts in creating it. When you can understand and admit the part you played in creating a problem, and still stand up for yourself, you are acting maturely and assertively.

A group of boys had just lost their basketball game because they missed the final shot. Each was yelling at the others and blaming someone else. Jason was blaming Salvatore for not passing the ball to him. Salvatore was blaming Patrick for blocking his pass. Patrick was blaming Dominic for not guarding him well enough. And Dominic was blaming Jason for a bad game plan.

The gym teacher blew his whistle loudly. "What's going on here?" he asked. Again, the boys all started talking at once, blaming each other. "You are all on this team together," said the teacher. "Each of you is responsible for part of the game. Each of you needs to tell me what you did that contributed to the problem."

Jason raised his hand. "I guess I was being selfish," he said. "I should have planned for Salvatore to pass the ball to someone else, but I wanted to make the winning basket." Then Salvatore spoke up. "If I had passed the ball to Jason right away like we'd agreed, Patrick wouldn't have been in my way. I was hoping I could make the basket myself." Patrick said, "I should have stayed out of the way when Salvatore didn't pass to Jason right away. I could have waited and given him more space. It was hard for Dominic to guard me when I was in the wrong place." Dominic said, "I shouldn't blame Jason for a bad game plan. He tried his best, but we just didn't make it work."

"That's mature talking," said the teacher. "You can each see the part you played in the problem. How do you feel about things now?" "I'm glad we're all on the same team," said Jason. "Let's try again, and we can do better next time."

For You to Do

Look at this picture of a problem situation. Then write what each participant is doing to contribute to the problem.

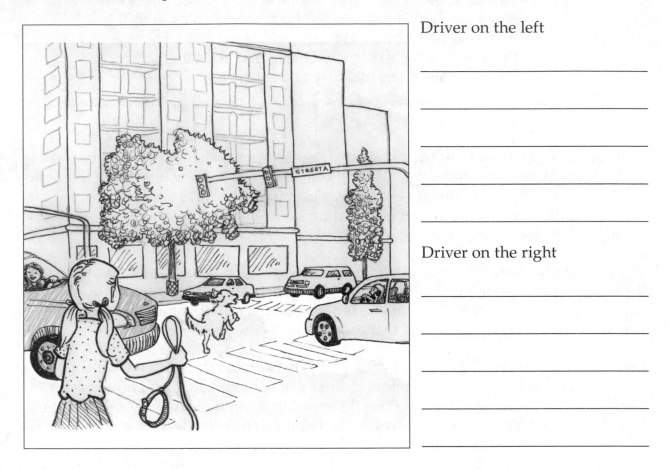

Driver on the left

_____

_____

_____

_____

_____

Driver on the right

_____

_____

_____

_____

_____

Dog owner

_____

_____

Dog

_____

_____

... *And More to Do*

Which seems easier at first: blaming someone else for a problem or admitting the part you played in creating it?

_____

_____

How does it feel to admit that you played a part in creating a problem?

_____

_____

Which action do you think helps solve a problem better: blaming others or admitting that you also played a part in it?

_____

_____

Describe a problem you are having between yourself and another person. Tell how each of you is contributing to the problem.

_____

_____

_____

Tell what you could each do to help solve the problem.

_____

_____

_____

Gina's grandma had more cats than anyone Gina knew. There were five altogether: two that stayed inside the house and three that stayed outside. When Gina visited her grandma, she liked to help her feed and brush the cats.

One day while Gina was playing with the cats, she told her grandma about a problem she was having with her best friend, Sean. Gina said that she and Sean were arguing all the time and she hated it.

"What do you argue about?" asked her grandma.

"We disagree about everything," said Gina. "And we never stop. We argue about the same things over and over again and never get anything solved."

"It sounds like you need some help from the five CATTS," said her grandma.

"The cats?" asked Gina. "How could they help us?"

Gina's grandma got out a piece of paper and wrote the letters C-A-T-T-S down the side. "If you can remember these five letters," she said, "then you can remember some good problem-solving guidelines." Next her grandma wrote a phrase to go along with each letter:

C—Calm down. "You have to be calm before you try to solve a problem or you'll be too angry to think clearly," she said.

A—Allow a good amount of time. "You have to allow enough time to really sit and listen to each other and work on the problem."

T—Think ahead. "If you think ahead about what you want to say, what is important to you, and how you might solve the problem, you will stick to the subject and solve things more quickly."

T—Talk nicely. "No name calling or saying mean things to the other person."

S—Stay focused on one problem. "Don't talk about other problems or things that happened days or weeks ago. Just stick to the one problem you have today."

The next time Gina and Sean were together, she told him about the five CATTS guidelines and he agreed to try them. They decided to meet on Saturday morning when they were both free. They both thought ahead of time about what they wanted to say. They both came to the meeting calm and relaxed. They decided to stick to the subject of which movie to see that afternoon. They chose nice words to express their thoughts and feelings. Because they took the time to use the CATTS guidelines, they agreed on a movie without getting into an argument. Then they both went to Gina's grandma's house to thank her and the cats for the great system!

For You to Do

Gina and Sean have a hard time remembering the CATTS guidelines. Help them solve this problem by writing one letter of the acronym CATTS next to each cat below. Then write the guideline that starts with that letter next to it. If you can, use a different color for each guideline.

... And More to Do

Help Gina and Sean some more by giving them extra ideas about how to use the guidelines.

C—Circle the healthy ways to calm down.

Take deep breaths.	Listen to peaceful music.
Relax your muscles.	Think about something that makes you mad.
Watch a scary movie.	Look at a pretty scene in nature.
Think about something relaxing.	Listen to people arguing.

A—Put a star by the situations that allow a good amount of time to try solving a problem.

Five minutes before school starts	When you have a day off from school
When you have time alone together	When your homework is finished
While the teacher is talking	While you are studying for a test
While you are going for a walk	While you are playing volleyball

T—Put a check mark by things that would be good to think ahead about before you try to solve a problem with someone.

How often the other person hurts you	What you don't like about the person
How you could agree	What part you played in the problem
What you would compromise on	How angry you are
What you want to say	What goal you both have

T—Underline the ways to **t**alk nicely to someone you are working out a problem with.

"I think I understand."   "You're stupid."

"I feel hurt when you say that."   "I want to listen to you."

"Dork."   "Please hear my side."

"I'm trying to see your side."   "You drive me crazy."

S—Put an X next to the lists that **s**tay focused on one problem.

Which movie to see, what time to leave, whose parents will drive

Which movie to see, last week when you lied to me, the time you didn't share

Whose house to play at, what to bring, if you can stay for dinner

Whose house to play at, the time you broke my watch, why you were rude to me

Whether to bike or hike, where to go, if we should ask another friend to come

Whether to bike or hike, the time you tripped me, the time you ignored me

Think about a problem you are having with a friend or relative. Describe how you could use the CATTS guidelines to work out your problem. Draw a picture of the two of you working out your problem.

Cool, Calm, and Confident

For You to Know

Brainstorming is a technique that helps you open your mind to new possibilities. When you brainstorm, you think of and try many solutions to a problem. If you work as a team using this technique, it will be easier to solve your problems with other people.

Ashley and Brad were looking at a model of the human brain in science class. "Wow," said Ashley, "that sure is a funny-looking place to hold all of our thoughts."

"It sure is," agreed Brad.

"Today we're going to talk about using your brain for a problem-solving technique called brainstorming," said Mr. Larson, the science teacher. "There are five steps to brainstorming," he said, and he wrote them on the board.

1. Describe a problem.

2. Without judging them, write down as many ideas as you can possibly think of to solve the problem. These ideas can be smart or silly, crazy or real.

3. Evaluate your ideas.

4. Choose one idea to try, and see if it works.

5. If it doesn't work, try another idea.

Then Mr. Larson wrote a problem on the board and told each pair of students to brainstorm solutions. Here is what he wrote:

My beard is too short. How can I get it to grow longer?

Here are the solutions that Ashley and Brad brainstormed:

Pull on it.

Water it.

Feed it.

Never get it cut.

Eat more protein.

Tape yarn on your chin (will look longer).

Ask the doctor.

Shave your head so all your hair comes out on your face.

Iron it to get the curls out.

When Ashley and Brad read their list, the class laughed. "Okay," said Mr. Larson, "if we evaluate the ideas, which one sounds like it might actually work?"

"Eat more protein," said Brad.

"Right," said Mr. Larson, "because hair is made out of protein. I'll try it for a week and see what happens. If it doesn't work, I'll choose another solution."

Brainstorming Solutions

For You to Do

Mr. Larson's class tried to solve a problem about growing a beard, but brainstorming can be used to solve problems between people, too. Each of the pairs of children below is having trouble solving a problem between them. Under the lightning bolt, write a list of ideas of how they might solve their problem. Write as many ideas as you can think of, and don't stop to judge them. They can be silly or smart.

... And More to Do

Practice brainstorming some more by writing as many solutions as you can to these problems. Put a star next to the idea that you would try first.

Your kitchen sink is overflowing.

_____

_____

_____

_____

You're standing at the bus stop, and a big wind starts blowing your homework papers all over.

_____

_____

_____

_____

You and a friend are in line at the store, and you realize that you don't have enough money for all your purchases.

_____

_____

_____

_____

Cool, Calm, and Confident

Now think of a problem you are having between you and another person.

Define the problem.

_____

_____

_____

Brainstorm solutions.

_____

_____

_____

Choose one to try, and tell what you think will happen when you try this solution.

_____

_____

_____

Tell which solution you would try next if the first one doesn't work.

_____

Share what you have written with the person you are having the problem with. Ask that person to try brainstorming with you, and write the results here.

_____

_____

_____

Choose one of your ideas to actually try. Write what happens here.

_____

_____

_____

Tell why you do or do not think brainstorming was a helpful way to solve this problem. If it was not helpful, tell what other problem-solving technique in this book you might try instead.

_____

_____

_____

For You to Know

When people use the technique of compromise, they can solve problems between themselves more easily. Compromise means that people agree to each give up a little of what they want in order to solve a problem. If people each give up a little, they will each get some of what they want, instead of one person giving up everything and the other person getting everything.

Maggie and Samaj were at a standstill in their argument. Neither would give in, and neither was happy with the way things were. They were standing at the locker they shared when Mr. Garcia, the principal, saw them. "What seems to be the matter, girls?" he asked.

"Samaj won't agree to decorate our locker with flowers," said Maggie. "Flowers are my favorite, and that's what I want." "Maggie won't agree to decorate our locker with animal pictures," said Samaj. "Animals are my favorite, and that's what I want."

Mr. Garcia looked from girl to girl. "If we want to get along with other people, we have to learn to compromise," he said. "Do you know what that means?" The girls shook their heads. "Compromising means you both agree to give up a little so you can each get some of what you want." "I'm not giving up my flowers," said Maggie. "I'm not giving up my animals," said Samaj.

"You're both standing up for yourselves, but you're not respecting the other's rights," said Mr. Garcia. "Are you two friends?" The girls nodded. "Do you care about staying friends?" They both nodded again. "Well, then, how could you compromise on decorating your locker?" The girls looked at each other. "Hmm," said Maggie, "I guess I could give up a little space. I don't need the whole locker for flowers." "Me, too," said Samaj. "I don't need the whole locker for animals."

"Good job, girls," said Mr. Garcia. "If you compromise that way, you each give up a little, but you each get some of what you want, and you still respect your friendship and each other's rights. You've solved your problem."

For You to Do

The Kids at Camp Compromise are learning to use compromise to act assertively. Help them each to give up a little and gain a little by writing a solution to their problem between the two of them.

Camper A says:

I want to sleep on the top bunk!

I want to swim.

I want to build the fire myself!

I want peanuts for a snack.

Camper B says:

I want to sleep on the top bunk!

I want to sail.

I want to build the fire myself!

I want raisins for a snack.

... *And More to Do*

Describe a problem you are having with someone right now.

_____

_____

_____

Describe what will happen if the two of you keep arguing about this problem and never come to an agreement.

_____

_____

_____

Draw a picture to go with this story.

Describe what could happen if the two of you find a solution to the problem by compromising. Be sure to tell what you give up and what you get, and what the other person gives up and gets.

_____

_____

_____

Draw a picture to go with this story.

Tell which way you would like your real story to turn out, and why.

_____

_____

_____

For You to Know

Some types of teasing are harmless and can be ignored or laughed at. Other types of teasing can cause harm and are not funny. When you learn to tell the difference between these types of teasing, you can have a better idea of when and how to act assertively.

Everyone gets teased by someone at some time in their lives. Your favorite aunt may tease you by saying that you are the most handsome boy or most beautiful girl in the entire world. Your brother may tease you by saying that you are a goofball. Your best friend may tease you about having a crush on someone in your class. You may tease other people, too. Maybe you tease your older sister about how much time she spends fixing her hair. Maybe you tease your friend about being a bookworm. You might tease your dad about being a couch potato when he watches TV for a long time.

These behaviors are playful teasing. These are the things that friends or acquaintances do or say to each other that are done out of friendship or fun. Playful teasing can be a way of interacting that helps us laugh at ourselves and at life.

Sometimes people are teased in a more harsh manner that doesn't feel playful or fun. Older children might tease younger children by pushing them down on the playground or stealing their backpacks. Larger children may tease smaller children by threatening to hurt them physically. Children might tease other children by calling them rude names or using profanity. Adults might tease children by calling them stupid or making fun of their physical problems.

These behaviors are harmful teasing, or bullying. These are the things that are done out of cruelty rather than out of friendship. When someone teases you in a harmful manner, it is important to know that this is behavior that must be stopped.

For You to Do

The children in the pictures below are all being teased. Look at what is happening in each picture and decide if the teasing is playful or harmful. If it is playful, color the smiling face below the picture. If it is harmful, color the frowning face below the picture.

... And More to Do

Describe a time when you were teased in a playful manner by someone you like who likes you, too.

_____

_____

How did you feel when you were teased this way?

_____

Were you able to laugh at yourself?

_____

Describe a time when you were teased in a harmful manner by someone who was being cruel.

_____

_____

How did you feel when you were teased this way?

_____

How did you make this person stop teasing you?

_____

Describe a time when you playfully teased someone you like and who likes you.

_____

_____

How do you think this person felt being teased?

_____

What did this person do or say?

_____

_____

Explain why you do or do not think that teasing like this is okay.

_____

_____

Describe a time when you may have teased someone in a harmful manner.

_____

_____

How do you think this person felt being teased?

_____

What did this person do or say?

_____

_____

Explain why you do or do not think that teasing like this is okay.

_____

_____

For You to Know

Some behaviors encourage people to tease you, and some behaviors discourage them from teasing you. When you treat yourself with respect, you usually choose to act in ways that discourage teasing. When you do not treat yourself with respect, you often choose behaviors that encourage others to tease you.

Thomas and Andrew were both new to the Morristown School. Thomas felt nervous about meeting all the new kids and teachers, but he treated himself with respect. Before going to school, he showered, put on clean clothes, stood up straight, and put a smile on his face. When he entered the classroom, he asked the teacher where he should sit and took his place quickly and quietly.

Andrew felt nervous, too, but he didn't know about treating himself with respect. That morning, he pulled on the wrinkled clothes he had worn the day before and he didn't brush his teeth. When he walked into the classroom, he sat far in the back and began to pick at his fingernails so he wouldn't have to look at anyone.

At lunchtime, Thomas asked the teacher to introduce him to some kids he could eat with. He sat up straight, spoke politely, and entered their conversation when there was a lull. When they talked about things he didn't know about, he listened quietly.

When Andrew entered the lunchroom, he walked hunched over with his head down. Because he wasn't looking where he was going, he bumped into a table, and his drink spilled. When that happened, he turned bright red and started to shake, which caused him to drop his whole tray. The kids at the table started laughing and called him a klutz.

Both Thomas and Andrew felt nervous about being new at school, but Thomas's behavior caused the other kids to accept him more easily. Andrew's behavior drew negative attention and made him an easy target for teasing.

For You to Do

Treating yourself with respect means treating yourself and your body in a caring way. Circle the respectful behaviors that will discourage teasing. Draw a line through the disrespectful behaviors that will encourage teasing.

Whine a lot.	Mind your own business.
Tell lies about yourself or others.	Get upset easily.
Do funny things with your body.	Tell the truth.
Act confidently.	Have a sense of humor about yourself.
Act like a know-it-all.	Have poor hygiene.
Put yourself down.	Don't let harmless teasing bother you.
Have good hygiene.	Tattle on others.
Stand up straight and smile.	Pick your nose.
Breathe evenly.	Make positive comments.
Let everything bother you.	Get enough sleep.

Behaviors That Encourage or Discourage Teasing

Activity 36

... And More to Do

Think of someone you know who gets teased harmfully by other kids. Write this person's first initial in the box below. Think about how this person acts around others. Write the things he or she does that might encourage teasing.

☐ _____
_____

Think of someone you know who rarely gets teased harmfully by others. Write this person's first initial in the box below. Think about how this person acts around others. Write the things he or she does that might discourage teasing.

☐ _____
_____

Tell about a time when someone teased you harmfully.

_____
_____
_____

Make a list of things you do that might encourage people to tease you.

_____
_____
_____

A Workbook to Help Kids Learn Assertiveness Skills

155

Make a list of things you could do that would discourage people from teasing you.

_____

_____

_____

Try some of the ideas from your list this week. Tell what happens.

_____

_____

_____

For You to Know

You can learn to handle teasing. There are certain things you can do that will help you feel better if you are teased and will also help you get the teasing to stop. Learning and practicing these behaviors is part of being assertive.

Lisa felt sad and frustrated. The other kids at school teased her nearly every day. Sometimes she came home from school in tears. One day her neighbor Julia saw Lisa crying as she was walking home. Julia was in high school. She was a friendly person, an A student, the vice president of student council, and a track star. She asked Lisa what was wrong.

"I am so tired of being teased," Lisa said. "I feel sad and lonely and angry. I wish the kids would stop, but they won't. I don't know what to do."

"I know just how you feel," said Julia. "When I was your age I was teased, too. But do you know what? Wishing won't make those kids stop, but I've learned a lot of tricks that can. Come on inside, and I'll write them down for you. I'll bet that if you try these ideas, they can help you, too."

Lisa sat at Julia's kitchen table and Julia told her how she used to be teased about many things—that she talked a lot, that she was very smart, and that her legs were very muscular. Julia said that when she learned to deal with the teasing, she also learned to use her unique characteristics to her advantage. Talking a lot helped her make friends, being smart helped her get good grades, and having strong legs helped her win awards for running. When she learned how to deal with the teasing, she felt better about herself and became a student leader.

Julia wrote down these ideas and showed Lisa.

How to Deal with Teasing

1. **Stick with friends.** Teasers usually tease when you are alone. If you see them coming, stick with your friends or stand near a teacher.

2. **Avoid teasers.** If you don't go near the teasers, they have less chance to bother you, and they will find someone else to tease.

3. **Ignore teasing.** Pretend you didn't hear the teasing and go on with your life. When teasers don't get a reaction from you, they usually stop. Tell yourself this rhyme: "If they are ignored, teasers get bored."

4. **Laugh.** If you learn to laugh with the kids who tease you, you can have fun instead of feeling upset.

"The first letters of each idea spell the word 'SAIL', said Julia. "Think of a sailboat floating peacefully through the lake. You can sail peacefully through teasing if you try these ideas."

Lisa tried the ideas the next week at school. At first it was hard to ignore the teasing, but when she did, the kids stopped. And at first she was afraid to laugh at herself; she thought the kids would only tease her more, but she found out they didn't. In fact, they stopped the teasing sooner. Lisa worked hard at handling the teasing and thought about how Julia had gotten past it and gone on to be happy and successful. She knew that if Julia could do it, she could, too.

For You to Do

You can remember Julia's ideas by drawing a picture of a sailboat in the space below. Then rewrite each idea below the picture.

S _____

A _____

I _____

L _____

... And More to Do

Make a list of things other people tease you about.

_____

_____

For each item on your list, tell which of Julia's ideas might help you deal with the teasing.

_____

_____

Which idea do you think would be easiest to try? Tell why.

_____

_____

Which idea do you think would be hardest to try? Tell why.

_____

_____

Try one of the ideas the next time someone teases you. Write what happens here. Write what you might do the same or differently if it happened again.

_____

_____

_____

_____

Cool, Calm, and Confident

Staying Calm to Handle Teasing

For You to Know

Staying calm can help you act assertively. When you feel upset, it is hard to think clearly and follow the guidelines for dealing with teasing. When you stay calm, you can think more clearly and follow these guidelines more easily. You can learn to stay calm by using both your body and your mind.

Lisa's friend Peter noticed that Lisa didn't get so upset about being teased anymore. It also seemed that the less upset she got, the less she was teased. Peter asked her to teach him how she stayed so calm.

"It's not easy at first," Lisa told him. "But after a while you get better at it. When I remember to use the SAIL ideas (**S**tick with friends, **A**void teasers, **I**gnore teasing, and **L**augh), they really work."

"I don't think I could do those things," said Peter. "When kids tease me, I get all red in the face and can't remember what to do. That seems to make them tease me even more."

"That used to happen to me, too," said Lisa. "Then Julia told me to use my body and my mind to stay calm, like this."

Use your body:

1. Relax your breath. When you breathe slowly and deeply, you feel calmer and can think more clearly.

2. Relax your muscles. You'll feel more peaceful inside and be more in control of what you say and do.

Use your mind:

1. Think of something that makes you happy. This takes your mind off the teasing and will make you smile.

2. Think of something funny. This takes your mind off the teasing and will make you laugh.

3. Think about someone who loves you. This takes your mind off the teasing and will make you feel warm and good inside.

Peter said he'd never remember all these things, so Lisa wrote them on a piece of paper, and Peter carried it in his pocket. He read it before school and after school and before he went to bed. Soon he started remembering the ideas without having to look at the paper.

For You to Do

From the list that follows, choose words that will help Peter use his body to stay calm when he is teased. Write these words inside the outline of his body. Then choose words that will help him use his mind to stay calm when he is teased. Write these words in his thought balloons.

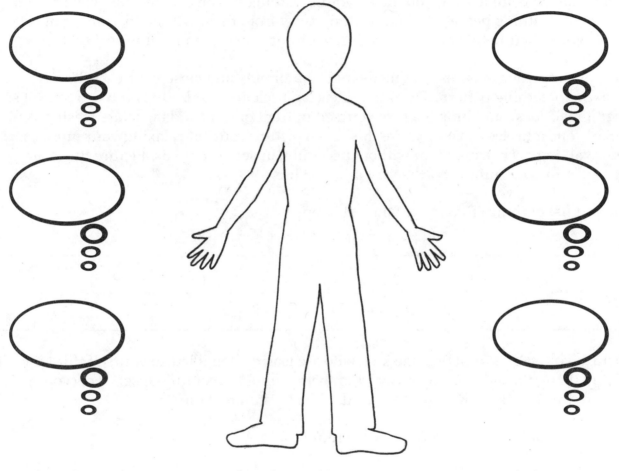

Fast breath	Relaxed muscles	Tense muscles
Peaceful muscles	These teasers are mean.	Shallow breath
I remember a great joke.	My dad loves me so much.	I love swimming.
I hate scary movies.	Slow, relaxing breath	My friend cracks me up.
My best friend thinks I'm cool.	Skateboarding is fun.	

... And More to Do

Try relaxing your breathing. Sit quietly and comfortably and close your eyes. Take a slow, deep breath, and then two more. Take a very quick, shallow breath, and then two more. Notice how you can control your breath by paying attention to it. Find a breathing pattern that feels calm and relaxing to you. Picture yourself in front of some kids who are teasing you. Relax your breathing as you picture this. Then picture yourself breathing peacefully and walking away from them without becoming upset or nervous. Picture this over and over in your mind, and then try it in real life.

Try relaxing your muscles. Sit quietly and comfortably and close your eyes. Use a relaxing breathing pattern. Think about each muscle in your body and try to relax it so that it feels loose and limp. Picture yourself in front of some kids who are teasing you. Relax your muscles as you picture this. Then picture yourself relaxing your muscles and walking away from them without becoming upset or nervous. Picture this over and over in your mind, and then try it in real life.

Make a list of things that make you feel happy.

_____

_____

_____

Picture yourself in front of some kids who are teasing you. Picture yourself thinking happy thoughts and walking away from them without becoming upset or nervous. Picture this over and over in your mind. Then try it in real life.

Make a list of things that you think are funny.

_____

_____

_____

Picture yourself in front of some kids who are teasing you. Picture yourself thinking about something that makes you laugh and walking away from them without becoming upset or nervous. Picture this over and over in your mind. Then try it in real life.

Make a list of people who love you.

_____

_____

_____

Picture yourself in front of some kids who are teasing you. Picture yourself thinking about someone who loves you and walking away from them without becoming upset or nervous. Picture this over and over in your mind. Then try it in real life.

For You to Know

There are times when being assertive all by yourself is not enough to protect you. Sometimes it is important to ask for help in order to keep yourself or others safe. Asking for help in times of necessity is not a sign of weakness, but an act of wisdom.

Sometimes, no matter how confident you feel, it is not wise to handle a situation by yourself. These are times when trying to stand up for yourself all alone will not be enough to keep you safe. At those times, it is important to find another person who is strong enough to help you.

Playful teasing is usually a situation you can take care of by yourself. You can also take care of some types of harmful teasing, depending on the circumstances. Other types of harmful teasing are not safe and may put you in real danger. At those times you must call for outside help.

It is important to be able to recognize situations when you cannot handle a situation assertively by yourself. If you think that you or someone else might get hurt in any of the following ways, it is best to act assertively by calling for help:

1. If someone is crying too hard to stop

2. If you think that someone is going to be physically hurt

3. If someone is physically hurt

4. If someone has a weapon of any kind, even if it is not being used

5. If something illegal is happening or is about to happen

6. If you feel any other kind of danger

For You to Do

Pretend that you are walking home from school. On your way, you see the following things happening. Look at each situation and put an H next to it if you think it is important to act assertively by calling for help. If you are not sure about your answer, talk it over with a grown-up before you decide.

Now look at the list of people to the center of the pictures. Decide whom you could call in each situation, and draw a line from that person to the situation. There can be more than one answer for each situation.

teacher

parent

any adult

school staff member

police officer

adult friend

grandparent

adult neighbor

school principal

... And More to Do

Describe what might happen in each of the pictures above if no one were called for help.

Picture 1

_____

_____

_____

Picture 2

_____

_____

_____

Picture 3

_____

_____

_____

Picture 4

_____

_____

_____

Picture 5

_____

_____

_____

Picture 6

_____

_____

_____

Write the names of adults in your life whom you could call for help if you needed it.

_____

_____

_____

Activity 40   Putting It All Together

For You to Know

This book teaches many ideas and skills for becoming assertive, including how to feel good about yourself, how to talk to and get along with other people, and how to handle yourself when others tease you. Assertiveness skills can be used alone or in different combinations, depending on the situation you are in.

The more you practice assertiveness skills, the easier they will get, and the easier it will be for you to know which ones to use at different times. Sometimes you may need to know how to handle a disagreement with a good friend, or you may need to know how to make a new friend. Sometimes you may need to know what to say to make conversation, or you may need to know what to say when someone treats you meanly.

Being assertive can help you in just about every situation in your life where you interact with other people.

For You to Do

Read the situations below. Tell how you feel and what you could do or say to act assertively in each case, standing up for your rights but respecting the rights of others as well. Think about all the ideas and skills you have learned in this book.

You are sitting alone on a bench outside of school, waiting for the bell to ring. Your backpack is next to you. Suddenly, a big kid from a higher grade runs by and grabs it. He throws it to another big kid, and they start playing catch with it. Your papers and books are falling out. How do you feel? How could you act assertively to help yourself?

_____

_____

_____

You are going on a picnic with your parents and some friends of theirs whom you have never met. The friends have a couple of kids your age, but you don't know them. When you get there, the kids are already swimming in the lake. You would like to swim, too. How do you feel? How could you act assertively to help yourself?

_____

_____

_____

You are sitting in a movie theater and the kids behind you are talking loudly. They are also throwing popcorn around, which is hitting you on the head. You can't hear the movie because they are so loud. How do you feel? How could you act assertively to help yourself?

_____

_____

_____

You are waiting in line at the drinking fountain. Another kid pushes in front of you and takes your place. How do you feel? How could you act assertively to help yourself?

_____

_____

_____

You are walking home from school. Three kids jump out at you from behind a car, pushing you down and kicking you. How do you feel? How could you act assertively to help yourself?

_____

_____

_____

You are called to the principal's office because someone told her that you were stealing supplies from the teacher's desk. You never did that or anything like it. How do you feel? How could you act assertively to help yourself?

_____

_____

_____

... And More to Do

Think of a situation in your life right now that you want to handle assertively. In the box below, draw a picture of yourself acting assertively. Add a conversation balloon that tells what you will say. Underneath the picture, describe what is happening and tell what you are doing to act assertively.

_____

_____

_____

Tell what you think the easiest part of acting assertively would be in this situation.

_____

Tell what you think the hardest part of acting assertively would be in this situation.

_____

Put your assertiveness plan into action, and tell what happens here.

_____

_____

_____

Lisa M. Schab, LCSW, is a licensed clinical social worker with a private counseling practice in the Chicago suburbs. She is author of twelve self-help books and workbooks for children, teens, and adults. Schab teaches self-help workshops for the general public and training seminars for professionals.

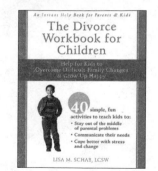